Black is a Color

Stanley Aaron Lebovic

Adina Rishe Gewirtz
editor

For questions, comments, information on scheduling an exhibit,
or purchasing any of the artwork, contact:
Stan Lebovic via email at: lebovic@blackisacolor.com

Black is a Color, Inc.
A non-profit organization
www.blackisacolor.com

In honor of

B-14529

my loving father

much more than a number,
too much for words.

My father's family circa 1937

Aunt Shayndle | My Bubbie | Uncle Aaron | My Zaide | Uncle Shlomo | Uncle Jack | Uncle Armin | My Father

Gassed upon arrival at
Auschwitz — Birkenau.
May 26, 1944

Collapsed and shot
on a death march.
Winter of 1945

Shot dead a few hours
before liberation.
Spring of 1945

Survived.
Liberated
May 1, 1945

A group of young boys was approached by an elderly gentleman...

The man stretched out his arm and began rolling up his shirt sleeve.

The boys stared as he revealed the presence of death camp numbers
tattooed upon his frail, slightly shaking arm.

He added the warning:

"Never forget what they did to us!"

And with that he bid them farewell.

- Actual incident as told by one of the boys in the group -

As the survivors dwindle in number, the responsibility to keep the memory alive falls squarely on our
shoulders. Without the visual impact of actual arms branded by the Nazi regime, it will become
harder and harder to keep the future generations from forgetting.

The following have given generously
in the hopes that the rest of us will never forget.

Dedication

שמים והארץ בְּהִבָּרְאָם בְּיוֹם

"God created the world to resemble the bottomless letter ה, thereby affording an easy descent for the wicked".*
However, it is the righteous few, who not only defy gravity, they invert reality in an attempt to save us all.

In a valiant effort to rotate the ה...

Albert Dov + Nancy
FRIEDBERG   have supported this publication in memory of...

Ricky + Dianna   &
ZAUDERER

Yonah ben Moshe
Zauderer
(1892-1942)

Sara bat Meir
Zauderer
(1895-1942)

As well as Sara's sister and her husband...
Hudie bat Moshe Kressel
(1899-1942)
Aaron ben Chaim Kressel
(1891-1942)

David **KAHANE**
& Michelle **FOX**
have supported this publication
in memory of...

73720
▼
Sam "Szmulek" Kahane
(1919-2000) *Auschwitz inmate (1942-1945)*

(Rashi, Genesis 2:4) In the Torah, the word בְּהִבָּרְאָם contains a diminutive letter ה, indicating that the word can be understood as: with the ה [the world] was created. The version illustrated above rotates the ה to remove the gaping bottomless abyss and reflect the desire for a world where all can find support and encouragement.

Contents

A Lasting Impression   14

The overall message of this collection is that life in a post-Holocaust world is drastically different than any existence man has experienced. What we have seen has altered our outlook on man and God forever.

Hide & Seek   16

The *Mezuzah* stands for God's constant watchful eye. Rendered as nearly imperceptible, or at best as part of the Swastika itself, the *Mezuzah* now represents a hidden God bordering on abject neglect, God forbid.

Turn the Page   18

The only prayers allowed through the heavenly gates are those drenched in tears. The eyes of the Jewish people run like rivers rushing towards the ocean. The seven seas overflow with every new drop. Our prayer books are soaked through and through. Is it time, perhaps, we dry our eyes and attempt to raise our voices?

Broken Glass   20

Amidst all the panes of glass that have come crashing down upon the Jewish people, how is it that the sound of a single glass broken under the wedding canopy can still be heard?

Destination Unknown   22

With both the duration and the final destination of their trip hidden from them, the deportees were credited for enduring every jolt, every jostle, every hum, and every screech along the endless railway.

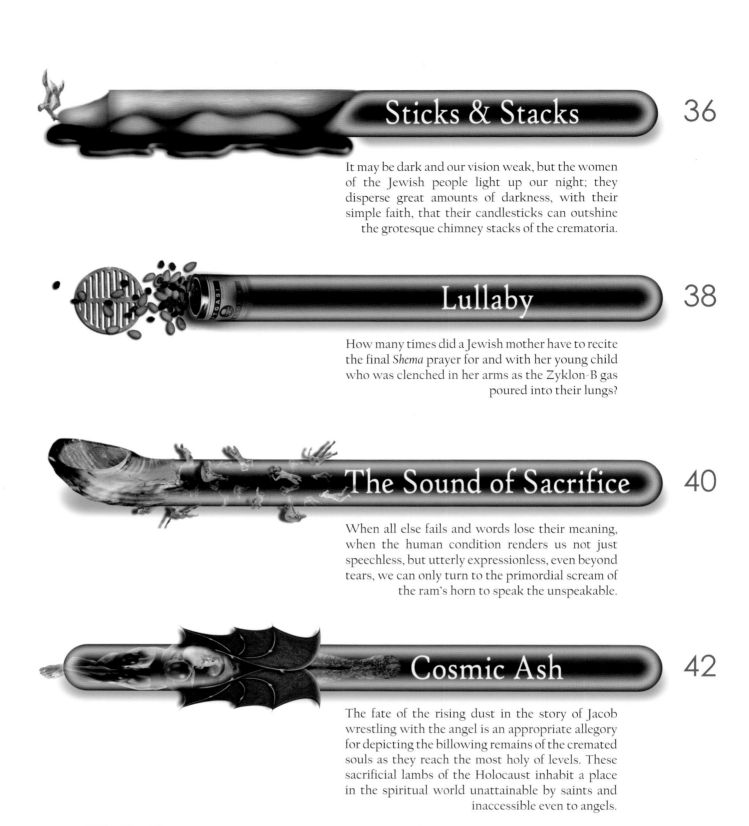

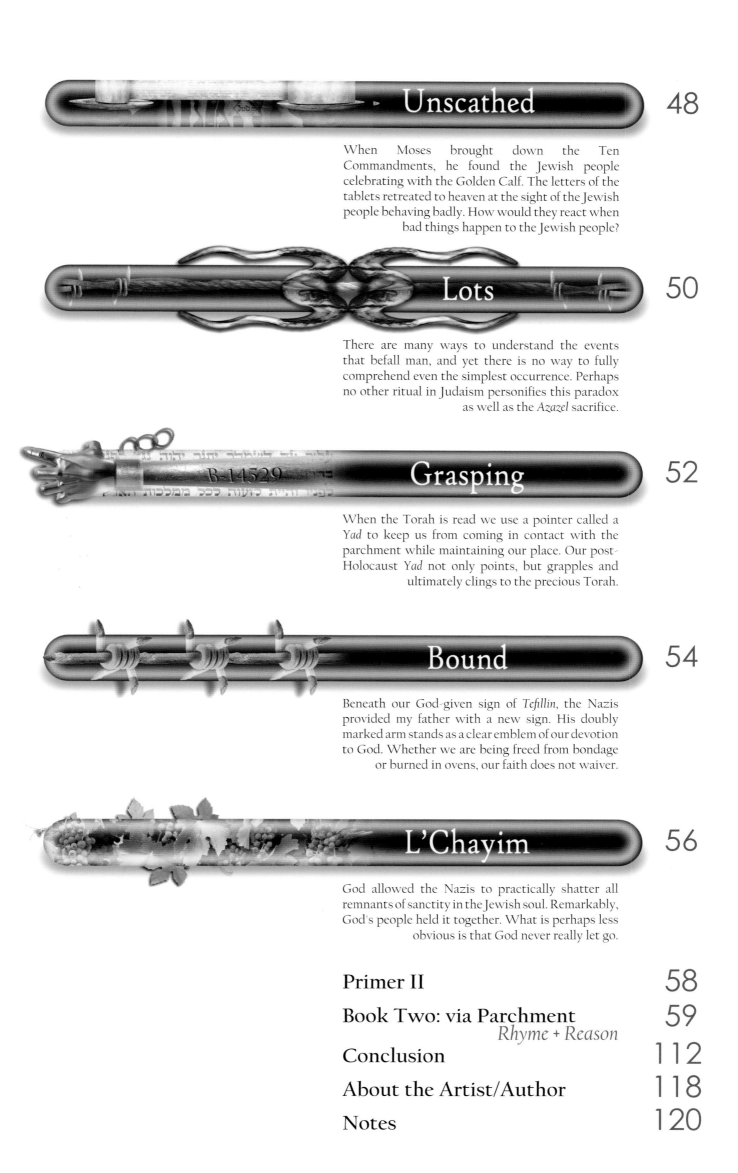

Forward

"Once upon a time there was a Holocaust...

As the son of a survivor of the Nazi concentration camps, I grew up hearing the first-hand testimony of a witness to humanity's darkest moment. Dr. Mengele supplanted Dr. Suess, and the Big Bad Wolf did a lot more than huff and puff. Sleeping with the lights on might keep the Boogie Man at bay, but nothing could beat back the horror of being tucked under the covers by an arm branded with death camp numbers.

As my father left my bedside and headed out the door, he would pause and turn back towards me. "Did you say your prayers?" he would invariably ask.

"Did I what?!"

How can you bequeath me such an encounter with the devil, and expect me to believe in a loving God? Do you really believe in everyone living 'happily ever after'?

Yet, somehow he did. He and countless other survivors experienced hell on earth and still found the strength to believe.

Growing up as the legacy of a survivor of the Holocaust had its unique challenges. Perhaps it was because he worked so hard to give me an idyllic childhood. Born and raised in suburban Los Angeles in the 1960s, I was nowhere near the war-torn world that ripped apart my father's family. One generation later, and all signs of the greatest cataclysm the world had ever known were safely tucked away.

I was safe ... but was I sound? Sure my crayon box had 64 colors and a built-in sharpener, but why did I only use the black crayon?

What happens when a generation grows up in comfort on the heels of so much horror? When the life you are bequeathed does not resemble the life you are leading, there exists a great inner dilemma. How do I make peace between my tranquil existence and my father's brutal past? The tranquility of my childhood only amplifies my ability to focus on the dilemma at hand. Moreover, I am raised to believe in the very God responsible for the atrocities of my father's generation.

It is this struggle to have faith in the midst of madness and the unique Jewish response to it that is the subject of *Black is a Color*, a series of art and prose that expresses how traditional Jews found — and still find — hope and faith in the midst of the deepest darkness. It is an attempt to illuminate man's post-Holocaust spiritual stature: a search for the happy ending.

Humanity lost 60 million people to the Holocaust, six million of them Jews. The themes of *Black is a Color* honor all of them with their universality, but they express most specifically images of traditional Jewish life.

The Talmud[1] teaches that a person who remembers the redemption from the Egyptian exile immediately before commencing to pray is worthy of an afterlife. Assuming eternal life is not earned on the cheap, what significance can be attributed to the juxtaposition of the redemption from Egypt and standing before God in prayer? It may very well be that serving God in the present requires being cognizant of our oppressive and ultimately redemptive past. Rabbi Yehudah Loew, known as the *Maharal* of Prague, discusses the importance of maintaining a focus on the exodus from Egypt in his work *Netzach Yisroel*. The *Maharal* contends that the only way to truly understand something is to comprehend its opposite. The long, dark exile experienced by the Jewish people can only be withstood in proximity to that great manifestation of salvation known as the Exodus. If we approach God without a recollection of what we have gone through, and how He has saved us, we cannot hope to survive.

The exodus from Egypt has served as the defining moment for the Jewish people for over 3,500 years. The Jewish people's steadfast focus on God's mercy has enabled them to survive destruction, inquisition and pogrom. Can the exodus, however, address a Holocaust? Is it possible that the 10 plagues and a splitting sea can no longer captivate a people who have inhaled the gas and been seared by the flames? Can a story extolling God's acrobatic benevolence in skipping over the Jewish homes during the killing of the first born, hold any allure for a people systematically selected for annihilation? Has the Jewish people's 'chosen' status merely put a price on their heads? And can the miracles experienced in their youth be recalled, let alone celebrated, to offer solace in their old age?

While the Exodus is central to Jewish faith, and always will be, the Talmud itself gives permission for children of the post-Holocaust world to focus on our most recent — and greatest — cataclysm in our search for salvation. Expounding on a verse in Jeremiah, the Talmud tells us: "While [memory] of the exodus from Egypt will never be uprooted, a [future] oppression will dominate [our perspective]".[2] There will be a single oppression at the end of days whose atrocities will be so great that the hearts and minds of the Jewish people will be forced away from a remembrance of a miraculous salvation and God's merciful ways, towards a ghastly encounter with God's burning rage.

In Egypt, the Jewish people became a nation and offered God the Paschal Lamb. In Nazi Germany, the Jewish people were the sacrificial lamb. Our status has changed dramatically, and along with it, so has every aspect of our lives.

This migration to a new focal point actually serves to alter the very fabric of our reality. A life lived in the glow of God's good graces has a very different hue than one lived in the shadow of His wrath. The *Maharal's* axiom — comprehension through contrast — would dictate that the horror unleashed upon the European continent in the middle of the 20th Century can provide the necessary backdrop whereby a clear view of the ultimate redemption can now come into focus. Exactly how humankind experiences a Holocaust and emerges with its faith not only intact, but enhanced, is the hidden miracle *Black is a Color* attempts to expose.

The early 19th century French painter Édouard Manet, whose artistic subject matter often portrayed the lighter sides of societal life and ushered in the colorful Impressionist movement, categorically claimed, "Black is *not* a color!" By contrast, the achromatic pallet of our post-Holocaust era limits our ability to portray life using anything but nihilistic images of the macabre. For us, black may as well be the only color!

Fortunately, trapped deep within black's drab facade exist all the colors of the rainbow. *Black is a Color* attempts to tap into that technicolor cornucopia and

reveal a rich-bodied color within the black, a color that adds depth and clarity to the portrait of our lives.

It is precisely from that dark, musty corner that the works of art and prose found in this collection emanate. They approach faith through confrontation rather than salvation. No sunflowers, no rainbows, no fuzzy warm feelings — instead we are thrown into the darkest corner of the universe, where, like a fungus, our faith can mushroom and develop. In this work you will not find inspirational tales of how divine providence miraculously saved an individual while destroying an entire town. Rather, it is the wholesale slaughter of town after town that will serve to eclipse any and all remnants of hope and direction. For what need is hope to a people who have already been saved? What good is direction when you have finally reached your destination?

The Jewish faith has an interesting custom for the burial of brutally victimized individuals. Traditionally, a strict regimen of cleaning and dressing the deceased must be adhered to. However, victims of violence are sent to their final resting place 'as is'. Their bloodstained garments and badly beaten corpses are left intact. No attempt is made to visually purify them. The rationale behind this shameful neglect is to invoke a heavenly reaction. By sending God's beloved back to Him in such a defiled state, we expect God to be moved to show mercy and redeem His children.

In a similar vein, the artwork developed for *Black is a Color* is meant to depict the heroic posture humanity has assumed in this post-Holocaust world and present it to both man and God. For man, it should serve as a reminder of the worth of his actions; for God, a testament to the worth of His creations.

and some people lived happily ever after"

Such were the bedtime stories I was raised on.

11

Primer I

"Come, let us
descend and
there confuse
their language".
Genesis 11:7
The Tower of Babel

"Language
lives from its
limits, drawing its
breath there, living
beyond its means".
Emmanuel Levinas

"Art picks up
where language
leaves off".
Susanne Langer

Faith in God boils down to one, incoherent equation:

$$G = g \neq e = G$$

(Where G stands for God, g for good, e for evil)

How do you articulate the incoherent? To share meaning, we must have words in common, and language builds a fence around our mutual understanding. This sound is gibberish; this sound makes sense. Speech lets us explore ideas within the safety of community. But what if the ideas that need exploring are the ones that so isolate us, so unmoor us, that they cannot be shared? How to express man's existential angst in language? When the pain of experience exhausts our words, we must turn to symbols, for only these can express the inexpressible.

The art in this book attempts to speak without words, to explore the unfathomable and react to it in color, line and form. The ideas embedded in these works are touched on only briefly in *Book One* to orient you, the viewer, for the experience of art should, first of all, be yours. Only once you have formed your own frame for these images do I offer the ideas that inspired me to create them, in a series of essays in *Book Two*, which begins on page 59. My hope is that together, with your understanding and then mine, this book can construct a dialogue between us, a fuller exploration of the colors that exist even in darkness.

Artist's confessions:

Life is lived one moment at a time, but it must be evaluated as a sum of its parts.

Here I tried to present the full time continuum rather than one specific moment, in an effort to broaden our perspective to include the cumulative experience of life lived as a whole.

My initial intention was that such a long view of a man's life would help soften the blow he must somehow endure within each maddening moment.

My efforts, however, were unsuccessful. In the final frame the dizzying spin of the pinwheel has resumed, but the menacing shadow remains.

In the final analysis, as uncomfortable as it may be, evil leaves a lasting impression.

Still

waters

run

deep.

Even the gentle spin of a child's toy seems to cast the long shadow of shattered youth and vanquished dreams. As a pinwheel spins in a gentle breeze, it casts a cooling shade over an unassuming face. Isolate the moment or calm the wind and a very different image appears.

The type of shadow cast upon mankind depends solely on perspective. In a world bound by time, we might have no choice but to see life as a series of isolated frames instead of an ongoing continuum. Frame by frame, life may be maddening, absurd, and full of unimaginable horrors. However, if we broaden our perspective, allow ourselves to see life as a total sum of its parts, we just might find some relief.

Relief, however, is not the focal point of *Black is a Color*. Rather, it is man's ability to maintain a belief in the ultimate goodness of God, in spite of the frame by frame evidence to the contrary that commands the attention of the art and prose found in this collection.

The spin has resumed however the shadow continues to cast its ominous influence.

(Commentary continues in Book Two on page 60)

A Lasting Impression

BEFORE

DURING

AFTER

Artist's confessions:

A few of the works in this collection come close to crossing the line. I believe this is unavoidable when dealing with such a significant topic. In this piece the quintessential icon of God's protection, the mezzuzah, is depicted as little more than an illusion. Its very existence is in question.

Originally this was disturbing enough, but after delving deeply into Judaism's outlook on divine providence, I was moved to take the image even closer to what might be considered the limits of acceptable imagery. The mezzuzah is in fact the very backbone of the swastika.

The braille letters on this page spell G O D.

Rav Joseph B. Soloveitchik (1903-1993) left us the most honest insights into the heart of one of Judaism's greatest minds. His eloquence in portraying the emotional angst and genuine separation anxiety inherent in man's distance from his Creator is unparalleled.

The Rav begins: "To be religious is not to be confused with living at ease, with unruffled calmness and inner peace. On the contrary, the religious life is fraught with emotional strife, intellectual tensions which ravel and fray its harmony. The religious experience not only warms, but also chills with horror ... Many a time man wonders whether or not God cares to intervene on his behalf. The tragic search for God, Who hides His face, is the great undertaking of man, and it frequently ends in despair and resignation. The Torah abounds in the complaints and pleas of the prophets who, even as they were committed to God and had unshakable faith in Him, were frightened by His absence from their midst ..."

(Commentary continues in Book Two on page 61)

Hide & Seek

Artist's confessions:

The overhead perspective utilized in this piece serves to combine the viewer's tears with those of the survivor.

While tears represent the proper expression man must assume when approaching God in prayer, our post-Holocaust existence may entitle us to turn the page on tears and find new footing for our dialogue with the Almighty.

The prayer book is turned to page 270 (spelled backwards, ע"ר to avoid writing the word for 'evil' — רע) it is symbolic in that It contains the memorial service from the holiday of Shavuoth. My father's family arrived at Auschwitz on a Friday night, Erev Shavuoth. His mother, brother, and sister were gassed to death that very night: the 49th day of the Omer.

After rivers of tears have overflowed pages of prayer,

it's time we dry our eyes and raise our voices.

Our view of God is clearly obscured. Our eyes go blind trying to catch a glimpse of the God we have fallen in love with. Try as we may, the world around us presents very little evidence that our Beloved still cares. His beneficent ways are shrouded in mystery and veiled in secrecy. The light of God's presence no longer shines warm and bright. In its place we must bear a cold and dark, almost blank, stare.

For centuries our prayers have struggled past our lips — resounded in echo — then returned to us as if unheard. This echoing silence fulfills the words of the Talmud, "From the day on which the Temple was destroyed all the gates of prayer have been closed ... save for the gates of weeping".

Unfortunately, tears are a commodity the Jewish people have in abundance. Our tear-drenched pleas have surely overflowed the heavenly gates and threaten to drown the Holy Throne.

Must we wait for the Third Temple before we can, once again, raise our voices in supplication? Is our present condition a result of the gates being closed, or have the gates closed due to our lack of approach?

(Commentary continues in Book Two on page 63)

Turn the Page

Of all the ideas set forth in this collection, the one contained in 'Broken Glass' remains the one I resort to the most in my personal struggle.

By nature I have a 'glass half-empty' personality. The idea that there is hope, even when the glass is completely shattered, is a difficult one for me to maintain.

It is therefore most fitting that I found it necessary to resort to the mythical Phoenix as the icon for this message.

Those who can stare down the futility of existence and constantly piece the broken shards together, finding a way to refill until overflowing, are what legends are made of.

Their first step as newlyweds is met with a shattering.

Before the bride and groom leave the wedding canopy, the groom lowers his foot with a defiant, almost victorious gesture, and breaks a fine crystal glass, whereupon, a roar of 'mazel tov' fills the hall. While their first step has stumbled, our attention is riveted on the couple's resolve to embark upon their journey in spite of the unavoidable challenges that lie in their path.

The origins of the broken glass date back to the fourth century. Our generation, however, knows that glass does not just break under the wedding canopy. On the night of November 9th, 1938 the Holocaust begins with *Kristallnacht*, a night of broken glass. It too ushers in a new beginning between a people and their God, a beginning of unimaginable challenges. And out of these challenges rise a people of mythical proportions. Like the phoenix, they must accept defeat before rising out of the ashes.

Amidst all the panes of glass that have come crashing down upon the Jewish people, how is it that the sound of a single glass broken under the wedding canopy can still be heard? Could the deliberate glass-breaking at a wedding help us cope with the belligerent night of glass breaking in the streets of Germany?

(Commentary continues in Book Two on page 64)

Broken Glass

Artist's confessions:

I focused this piece on the details of the individual railroad ties in an effort to emphasize the journey instead of the blurry and dark, unknown future.

A journey, it turns out, that shares many characteristics with Abraham's personal deportation from his homeland of Haran.

I was so preoccupied, however, comparing Abraham's journey to that of European Jewry, that I neglected to realize how applicable the message is to all our lives.

It was my daughter, Shayna who pointed out the glaring similarity between Abraham's trek towards the unknown and life's constant unfolding towards an uncertain future.

With every 'click' and every 'clack' of the endless track.

When God instructs Abraham to leave his homeland, He specifically leaves out a very important detail. God neglects to tell him where he is to go. Instead, God assures Abraham that He will eventually show him his destination, but for now he is simply to leave.

By hiding the destination from Abraham, God is allowing him to focus his service on the task at hand. From the moment Abraham sets out on his journey he is fulfilling God's commandment in its entirety.

Abraham's children truly walked in his footsteps when the Germans loaded them into cattle cars on their way to concentration camps. They had no idea where they were going or how long they would have to endure the ghastly conditions of overcrowded cars.

As a result, every 'click' and every 'clack' of the endless track of rail mattered. They were credited for enduring every jolt, every jostle, every hum, and every screech along the way. Not a single discomfort went unnoticed nor was left bereft of meaning.

(Commentary continues in Book Two on page 67)

Destination Unknown

Artist's confessions:

I have more recurring nightmares than I have dreams. Chief among them is the struggle to navigate through a passageway which is far too small to manage.

My nocturnal neurosis probably has something to do with Rav Hirsch's metaphor of the wine press.

This illustration employs a rather benign substitute for the wine press, the cocoon. I apologize for that. I do not mean to minimize the trauma, I simply choose to focus on the way they emerged rather than on how they endured.

A holy nation was herded like animals and confined like sardines, but ultimately they emerged like heavenly angels.

Pressed to the limits ...and beyond.

King David opens three of his Psalms with a reference to what some believe is a musical instrument, the *gittis*. However, Rav Samson Raphael Hirsch believes that *gittis* actually means a wine press. The wine press is a somewhat ghastly, torturous device used to crush the delicate fruit of the vine and thereby forcibly extract its sweet nectar.

The *gittis* is used as a metaphor for man's ability to evolve. It is only through the great wine press of life that man can transcend his prosaic destiny and become, "only slightly lower than the angels". The trials and tribulations that befall man on this earth work as a human press to extract and refine the latent abilities lurking within his degenerate exterior.

In the cattle cars, the Jewish people were packed like the proverbial sardine, compressed to standing room only conditions for days and sometimes weeks on end, as they were extracted from their homes and sent to the camps. The winepress was no longer a metaphor, but a harsh reality.

(Commentary continues in Book Two on page 69)

Confine, Refine, Define

Artist's confessions:

This was by far the hardest piece to conceive. The images of the Covenant are so drastic and their counterparts in the camps are so heart-wrenching that I had a very difficult time boiling it all down into a powerful visual.

I still would like to find a way to include the correlation between the divided animals of Abraham's covenant and the selection process of the SS Soldiers.

You will notice, however, that I try and maintain a single focus in my pieces, resulting in an almost iconic representation of the message. Incorporating the 'selection process' would dilute the central impact of the smoking furnace and the lit torch.

In order to find the brightest light, one must look in the darkest corner.

'The Covenant Between the Parts' was initiated because of Abraham's concern that subsequent generations may not live up to the high standards of a chosen people. The Covenant assured Abraham that God's promises would never be revoked, rescinded or otherwise altered.

Between the parts, Abraham finds consolation in the apparition of a, "smoking furnace and a lit torch". Might a 'smoking furnace' be the perfect symbol for a gas chamber? A 'lit torch' a crematorium?

Abraham sees that millions of his great-granddaughters will be forced into smoking furnaces and gassed to death with their offsprings clenched in their arms. In this vision there cannot be any consolation.

Not in the vision, but perhaps in the sound. It is not what Avraham saw that put him at ease, it was what he heard. He heard, not the cries of his people, but their voices. He heard their voices rise from the *smoking furnace* in a chorus that would make the famous phrase '*Na'aseh VeNishma*' pale by comparison. His children entered the gas chambers with the song 'I Believe' emanating from their vocal cords.

(Commentary continues in Book Two on page 76)

The Covenant

Artist's confessions:

Sometimes the best way to portray something is not to. The sight of actual suffering can trigger a defense mechanism and block any feelings of empathy.

By dealing with the abandoned suitcases rather than their cremated owners, we allow ourselves a degree of attachment and it becomes possible for empathy to sneak up on us.

'Baggage' was one of the only pieces whose art preceded its prose. After viewing the completed work I began to question why earthly possessions should strike such a sensitive cord. Certainly it is man's spirit, not his left-over belongings, that matters most, or is it?

The ravens (in flight) provide contrast to the stranded luggage. For a deeper understanding see the Talmud, Eruvin 22a.

With

all

our

possessions.

With little or no warning, the Nazis rounded up their captives and herded them onto the cattle cars. If a family had time, they threw what they could into a suitcase and held on to hope that this was relocation rather than extermination.

While the graphic images of the deceased, piled one on another, may be too much for us to process, the photos of confiscated personal effects provide a less confrontational glimpse.

The image of one's belongings abandoned by the tracks conjures up a sense of empathy for its owners. These people hoped against hope that they would still have a need for their precious few earthly possessions. Instead, their possessions outlived them and now stand orphaned in an empty railway station.

The Talmud tells us, "Regarding the righteous, their property is more precious to them than their own bodies". Similarly the advice is given, that when traversing through thorns one should roll up his trousers, for while the skin will heal, the cloth will not.

(Commentary continues in Book Two on page 78)

Baggage

Artist's confessions: I find the juxtaposition of diverse images extremely potent in bringing out a message. Here I lined up the fence posts with the music bars and was able to stay true to both the sheet music and the electric fence.

This piece depicts the barbed wire fence of a concentration camp supporting the musical notes of 'Treulich Ge-fahrt', a famous composition by the German composer Richard Wagner (1813-1883).

It is said that Hitler would carry a sheet of Wagner's music wherever he went. Wagner himself was a rabid anti-Semite.

'Treulich Ge-fahrt' is better known, throughout the western world, as the wedding song, 'Here Comes the Bride'.

Whether in B-flat or A-sharp...

it is terribly off-key.

One of the most surprising components of the Nazi regime is that Germany was a nation on the cusp of cultural aristocracy. We aren't talking about a nation of savages. We are dealing with the brightest and most talented of peoples. How do we get genocide from the same hands that painted masterpieces, composed symphonies, and gave the world scientific breakthroughs of the highest order?

The sensitivity and sophistication required to create things of beauty does not seem to lend itself to acts of savagery.

Was Nazi Germany an anomaly? Or does it tell us more about human nature than we care to know?

According to Rav Soloveitchik, man's creative nature is none other than his *Tzelem Elokim*, or divine spark. Man's creativity mimics the creative component of the ultimate Creator and it is this emulation of God's creative nature that sets us apart from the animal kingdom.

Creativity, as the most godly of all human endeavours, is precisely the trait most likely to instill, in man, a tendency towards a god complex. As a god among mere men, the creative genius becomes the savage beast.

(Commentary continues in Book Two on page 83)

Culture Shock

Artist's confessions:

This piece was originally illustrated six feet in length. I had included a bloodthirsty image rising from the ground at the bottom of the canvas, (see graphic on page 85). I wanted to make sure that the message concerning the ground's wrongdoing would come across.

The piece, however, lacked a specific focus, and I reworked it to the current version.

Now the overall composition works to support the message of culpability. The aerial perspective of the train arriving at the concentration camp begins to give way — allowing the tracks to contort as they dangle and drip with guilt.

God does not want to punish us, and we must not let Him.

Silence is not always a virtue. When Cain slew his brother, we find that the ground opened its mouth wide and received his brother's blood. However, while the ground strove to conceal, the blood did what it could to reveal. Abel's blood refused to accept its fate. It took exception to the natural order of events. The blood's outrage may have originated from the ground, but it is ultimately directed towards God.

Is this not blasphemous? Such insubordination could set a dangerous precedent. Yet God heard the cries of the blood, punished the ground, and brought justice based on those cries.

Abel's blood teaches us not only to renounce evil, but that the fight against evil must be waged at heaven's gate. By rejecting the passive, obedient ground, and accepting the rebellious insubordination of Abel's blood, God in essence has granted man the right to rebel against Him!

The human condition is not a blessing from God: it is a curse. As God had told Cain, "... sin rests at the door. It desires you, yet you can conquer it".

(Commentary continues in Book Two on page 85)

Apathy

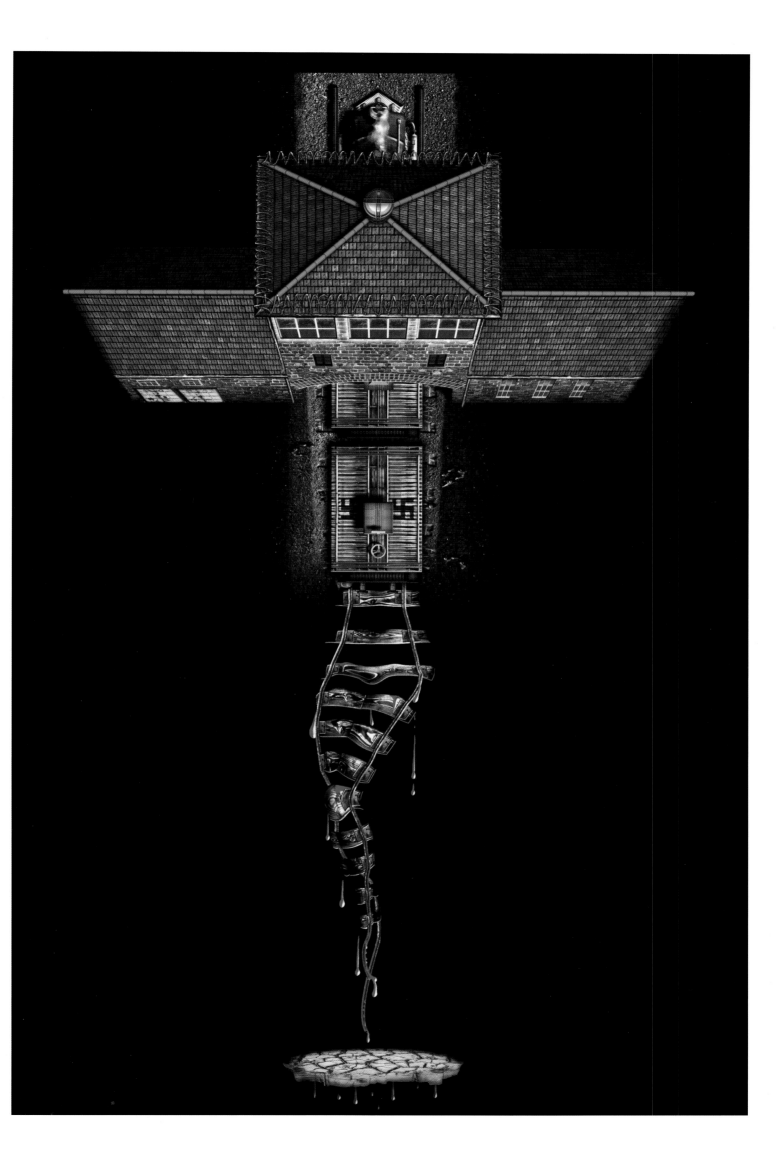

Artist's confessions:

The presence of the lulav and a hint of the shadow of the palm-leaves above, is meant to indicate that this visual is not a post-holiday portrait, where such usage of the etrog might be tolerated, rather it is a blatant disgrace and misappropriation of a precious commandment to wave the four species.

To me, the visual of such a coveted object, the etrog, carelessly thrown in a bucket, clearly illustrates the round-up and confinement of a beautiful nation. If the fruits weren't so plump they might also conjure up images of the heaps and heaps of dead bodies.

The numbers stamped on the various citrons are the numbers my father and his family were tattooed with.

Life and death were no longer ordained by the hand of God,

but fated by the finger of monsters.

While the pious carefully inspect every detail before selecting an *etrog* for the holiday of *Succoth*, the Nazis made *their* selections in an almost arbitrary manner.

My father was an inmate of Auschwitz-Birkenau, where he experienced the selection process first hand. The Nazis chose the holiest days of the Jewish calendar to conduct their selections. On *Rosh HaShana*, my father was tall enough; *Kol Nidre* he was strong enough; by *Succoth* none of that mattered — my father was sent to the left.

On the way to their deaths, some 5,000 boys in his selection sang *Ani Ma'amin/I Believe* in unison and spoke of loved ones they hoped to be reunited with in the afterlife. In my father's case he was fortunate that at the last minute a top SS officer happened to notice that a few of the boys still had some strength left in them, and pulled them from the others.

When the Nazis meted out death sentences with the wave of a finger, they robbed mankind of faith in an orderly universe. This was the ultimate profaning of the sanctity of life.

(Commentary continues in Book Two on page 88)

Still Life

Artist's confessions:

The act of lighting requires little effort. A simple strike, a wave of the hands, and a short blessing. It is the message which carries the great effort. And never before has that message been so difficult to deliver.

This piece juxtaposes our deepest hopes with our darkest horrors. I have set the table but I was unable to polish the silver. Perhaps fittingly, perhaps due to my lack of artistic ability, whatever the reason, try as I may, the melting chimney stacks refused all attempts at beautification.

The Sabbath table in this work, as well as post-Holocaust life in general, must support both the holy and the horrifying, the glorified alongside the grotesque.

Every
Friday night
it is *her*
candles that burn
but *their*
chimney stacks
that melt.

Judaism seems to be locked in a constant downward spiral. Every generation seems to fall short of its predecessor — both in spirit as well as deeds. The phrase in Rabbinic literature is, *Hitkatnut hadorot.* While Darwin's *Theory of Evolution* sees physical organisms racing towards greater and greater levels of perfection, Judaism acknowledges a palpable spiritual weakening.

The light of open miracles, prophets, and oracles has been blotted out by pogroms, long exiles, and concentration camps. "The Eternal shall smite thee with madness, and blindness, and disquietude of heart: And thou shalt grope at noon-day, as the blind gropeth in thick darkness". It is bad enough that we exist in a thick darkness, but what is worse is that we are blind as well. Our spiritual vision is without night-vision, sonar, or radar.

It may be dark and our vision weak, but the women of the Jewish people light up the night and disperse great amounts of darkness in their simple faith that their candlesticks can outshine the grotesque chimney stacks of the crematoria.

(Commentary continues in Book Two on page 90)

Sticks & Stacks

Artist's confessions:

In this portrayal, the young woman/mother image is a photo of my eldest daughter. She is named after my grandmother, Frayda who entered the gas chamber with her youngest children, on the night before Shavuot in 1944 upon their arrival at Auschwitz Many a night as a young child I was put to sleep to the Yiddish lullaby, Rozhinkes-mit-Mandlen (Raisins and Almonds), which speaks of a mother's hope for her only son's future: "Someday you will trade in raisins and almonds...that will be your calling. Sleep now, little one, sleep". Ironically, the aroma of the poisonous gas, Zyklon-B, is said to resemble that of almonds.

They were her last words, dare I utter them even once, let alone three times a day?

How many times did it occur, that a mother had to recite the final *Shema* prayer, for, and with, her young child who was clenched in her arms as the Zyklon-B gas poured into their lungs.

Often the first words a Jewish child is taught, and the last prayer on the lips of a Jew before his soul departs, is the proclamation of his unwavering belief in one God through the recital of the *Shema* prayer. Yet, in spite of the *Shema's* lofty stature, it is rather commonplace. It is to be found on the lips of observant Jews at least three times each and every day.

Should there be such a mingling of the sacrosanct and the mundane in man's actions? Can six words be so extraordinary on the one hand and so ubiquitous on the other? Should I be freely allowed to utter the same declaration as a young mother being gassed to death while holding her infant child? How dare I? Yet my earliest memories are of my father putting me to bed by placing my hand on the *mezuzah* on my room's door-post, covering my eyes, and there, teaching me to recite the *Shema*.

(Commentary continues in Book Two on page 91)

Lullaby

Artist's confessions:

I struggled with this piece the longest. As a result of that prolonged development process I've come to appreciate this image more than the others.

Finding an appropriate image to place within the gas chamber as an expression of what took place within its walls, was no small feat.

The ram's horn made a lot of sense on paper, but what shape and form it should take to express the inexpressible was the product of many revisions.

When I finally hit upon the exploding rib-cage, and could successfully pose the horn's mouth in a gasping posture, I was personally satisfied.

The surreal addition of human figures focus's the horn's angst upon the human condition.

When the indescribable becomes inexpressible.

When all else fails and words lose their meaning; when the human condition renders us not just speechless, but utterly mute, even beyond tears; we can only turn to the primordial scream of the ram's horn to say the unsayable. We take comfort in knowing that our inarticulacy is not the end of the line.

Rav Abbahu said, "Why do we blow a ram's horn? The Holy One, blessed be He, said: 'Sound before Me a ram's horn so that I may remember on your behalf the binding of Isaac the son of Abraham'".

After witnessing six million bindings, and no sign of an angel preventing the binding from turning into a sacrifice, does the ancient story still resonate with value? How can the ram's horn continue to communicate on our behalf?

This conundrum is what gives the ram's horn its special quality. It is a signpost directing our attention to the reality of life. Our inability to fully comprehend the world we live in is a natural component of the human condition, as is our desire to continue to seek explanations.

The ram's horn both heralds and wails.

(Commentary continues in Book Two on page 92)

The Sound of Sacrifice

Artist's confessions:

Years before I began working on this collection, I was asked to design a Holocaust Memorial. The battle between Jacob and the Angel was an obvious place for me to look for ideas.

Because of its popularity, I wanted to bring a fresh perspective in recreating such a familiar scene. Therefore I rendered the angel slightly demonic, and presented them from an aerial perspective.

By extending the chimney up towards the viewer, the smoke and ash can billow directly into our faces, and the agony on Jacob's face can look to us, the future, for salvation. Jacob's partial incineration represents the 1/3 of the Jewish people who were killed

The gate
of the
righteous
stands
atop
the stack
of the
chimneys.

As the transports unloaded their human cargo at the gates of the camps, the smell of death filled the lungs of the new arrivals. Orange flames, black smoke and grey ash could be seen billowing out of the chimneys and rising to the heavens.

Upon arriving at Auschwitz-Birkenau, my grandfather, Dov Lebovic, a Czechoslovakian veteran of World War I, turned to his sons and warned them that the odor in the air was unmistakably that of burning human flesh.

The rising ash hearkens back to a biblical encounter where dust rose heavenward. The fate of the rising dust in the story of Jacob wrestling with the angel is noted by the commentators. However, it more aptly serves as an allegory for depicting the billowing remains of the cremated, sacrificial lambs of the Holocaust. It is this precious ash which rose to the heavens and reached the throne of God.

Indeed, in a macabre gesture, Adolf Eichmann, the logistics supervisor for the mass exterminations, posted a sign above the crematorium at Birkenau: "This is the gate of the Lord into which the righteous will enter".

(Commentary continues in Book Two on page 94)

Cosmic Ash

Artist's confessions:

While my intention in this piece is to compare the encounter experienced by Moses at the Burning Bush with the encounter experienced by the entire Jewish nation in the Holocaust, I in no way mean to contrast the two. Both are examples of the finite struggling to comprehend the Infinite. What was a lowly bush is now an electrified fence; what were thorns are now barbs; instead of pretty flowers hang yellow stars.

It is this solidarity between events that compelled me to illustrate Moses's shoes turned away from the bush, in compassion rather than confrontation.

Technically this may not be incorrect, for Moses was turned away when he was told to remove his shoes.

Why did God speak out of a thorn bush? For it resembles a fence.

(Exodus Rabbah 2:5)

The Torah offers us a front row seat to the monumental, first encounter between God and His most accomplished servant, Moses. The story of the *burning bush* holds fascinating insights into the nature of our relationship with the Creator. Specifically on areas of suffering and survival, this maiden rendezvous speaks volumes to our post-Holocaust existence.

In our most recent brush with total annihilation, an eerie symbol provides an uncomfortable link back to the thorn bush. The Nazis were exceedingly orderly, and maintained warehouses of artifacts left over from their millions of victims. One such stockpile that evokes visceral emotions are the piles upon piles of shoes.

In Moses's encounter, God commands him not to approach the bush, and to remove his shoes. The ground beneath his feet may be rocky, but it is holy.

Similarly, the concentration camps can stand as an almost insurmountable obstacle in man's quest for faith. A forbidden wasteland for the spiritually thirsty. Yet it is precisely in this grotesque terrain where we must journey, unprotected, vulnerable and without support.

(Commentary continues in Book Two on page 95)

On Holy Ground

Artist's confessions:

In my creative process I initially began with the illustrative component. I soon found that the writing process actually brought me to a deeper understanding of the subject at hand and invariably I had to render a deeper and more profound visual.

In this piece I originally was interested in simply displaying blood-stained fringes, and I was content with bringing across the idea that a major article of clothing for the religious Jew is no longer pristine white. Once I began unravelling the techelet component, I realized that the image had to represent the link, established by the techelet, between the earth and the heavens, between man and his Creator.

Techelet will remain lost as long as man remains color-blind.

According to the commandment, the corners of a four-cornered garment must be finished with eight fringes: *Tzitzit.* A single thread is dyed with the blood of an animal to the color of *techelet*, a hue which turns out to be quite elusive.

The dye necessary to generate *techelet* has been lost to the world since the destruction of the Second Temple. Rabbi Yitzchak Luria maintains that the addition of *techelet* to our otherwise all-white fringes is only necessary while the Temple stood.

There is no fear that apathetic modern man will be so proactive that he will require the *techelet* to rein him in. Until society finds the strength to take a real stand against evil, there is no need to remind us that we are but a speck in the infinite expanse, for we fail to act like anything but.

Indeed, our post-Holocaust existence requires a *techelet* of a different shade. While the bluish *techelet* of the Torah resides at the far end of the color spectrum, holding our passions in check, our *techelet* might as well be fashioned from fiery red, bent on igniting our dormant inferno within.

(Commentary continues in Book Two on page 98)

Bloodshot

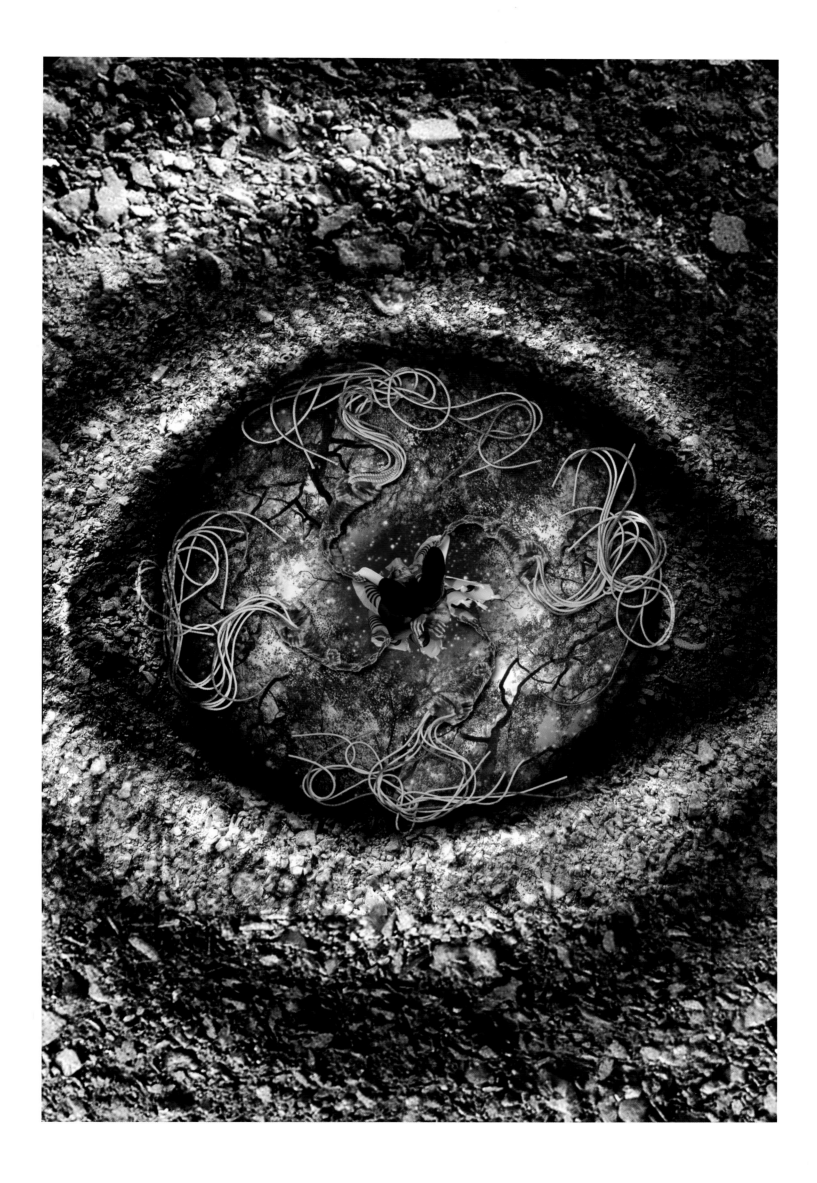

Artist's confessions:

For this work I opted for the rare form of hagbah, (lifting of the Torah) whereby the Torah is grasped with hands twisted and raised so that the words are visible to the onlookers and not to the one lifting.

Visually, this allowed a better view of the stubborn letters refusing to burn, but there was another motivation as well.

I remember my father telling me that his brother, Shlomo (whom I was named after), was the strongest of the brothers. He would marvel at Shlomo's ability to show evidence of his power by performing this difficult form of hagbah.

The words right between the eyes read, "He is the faithful God, Who safeguards the covenant".

When the

nation

sins,

the letters

retreat

to heaven.

However...

The Torah tells us that when Moses ascended the mountain to wrestle the law away from the celestial beings he seemed to tarry. With what appears to be tremendous haste, the Jewish people waste no time appointing a new leader; this time however, it is an idol!

As Moses descends with the Tablets, the intensity with which the people are celebrating their newfound deity stuns him, and instead of delivering the precious Tablets of the Law, he decides to shatter them.

The *Midrash* takes the blame slightly off Moses's shoulders by claiming that the hewn letters beat a hasty retreat at the sight of the spiritual carnage. With the letters on their way back to heaven, the blank stone grew exceedingly heavy and could no longer be held.

When the nation sins, the letters bid them farewell. However, when sins are committed against the nation, even when the very parchment they are written on is being consumed, the letters remain as beacons of hope and guidance.

(Commentary continues in Book Two on page 101)

Unscathed

Artist's confessions:

You may not know it by looking at it, but this piece and its associated prose, in my opinion, provide the safest refuge from the existential angst brought on by the Holocaust.

The artwork does what it can to link the Azazel sacrifice with the human sacrifice of the Holocaust: The Temple floor is strewn with poisonous canisters, the horns are twisted into a swastika and the barbed wire morphs into the crimson thread of forgiveness.

What the artwork fails to do is tap into the utter absurdity of the Azazel ritual. The injustice, the arbitrariness, the deliberately mixed message of Azazel are all absent in this rendition. To do justice to the idea, the art should find a way through confrontation to provide comfort.

"And the goat, designated by lot, for *Azazel* shall stand **alive** before God".

There are many ways to understand the events that befall man, and yet there is no way to fully comprehend even the simplest occurrence. One of the starkest examples of the incomprehensible, of course, is the Holocaust. Many seek answers to the dilemma that is genocide. Ultimately however, all explanations will fall short, all tongues become tied, and lips sealed, at the apprehension of such calamity.

At the height of the Yom Kippur service, two goats are prepared as offerings, but only one is offered in the Holy Temple. The other is selected by lottery to be sent into the desert, as an offering to 'Azazel'. The most obvious message would be that life and death are arbitrary. These goats are identical, yet by the luck of the draw, one serves God while the other does not.

The Chassam Sofer makes matters worse by pointing out that the goat who is laden with the nation's sins and whose lot is the desert, is actually granted an elevated state over his twin. "And the he-goat designated by lot for *Azazel* shall stand alive before God". The one, full of sin, shall remain alive, and for the time being, well.

(Commentary continues in Book Two on page 102)

Lots

Artist's confessions:

I almost did not include this image, because it has crossed the line. I in no way want to give the impression that the clinging hand is actually trying to mutilate or destroy the precious text it is employed to point at.

The only reason I reintroduced this piece is because I feel the title helps bring it back from the brink. 'Grasping', shows that the intent is to never let go no matter how difficult it may be. The tougher the trial the tighter our grip must become.

The portion of the Torah depicted is from the 'Tochecha' (rebuke). An especially hard section to read through, and, I am sure, an even harder section for God to write.

A firm *grasp* is not a prerequisite for our tight *grip*.

"Whatever you do, do not say: 'water, water'!"

That was the only advice offered by the great Rebbi Akiva to his three fellow travelers as they entered the *Pardes* (orchard). As it turns out, that was not quite enough to protect them from harm. Ben Azzai took one look and perished. Ben Zoma went mad, and Aher (Elisha ben Avuyah) lost his faith.

What or where is *Pardes*? It is not clear, but consensus says it was a state of spiritual enlightenment. The four men embarked upon a journey beyond the limits of human comprehension. As it turns out, it was a suicide mission (physically, mentally or spiritually) for all but one of them. Only Rebbi Akiva was able to return in peace. The specific details surrounding this ill-fated expedition are few and cryptic.

In terms of grasping life's meaning while maintaining a grip on reality, Ben Azzai's grasp exceeded his grip, Ben Zoma's grasp rivaled his grip, Aher's grasp loosened his grip, while Rebbi Akiva's tight grip remained unaffected by his ability, or inability, to grasp at all.

(Commentary continues in Book Two on page 104)

B-14529   Grasping

והיה אם לא תשמע בקול יהוה אלהיך לשמר

לעשות את כל מצותיו וחקתיו אשר אנכי מצוך

היום ובאו עליך ... הקללות האלה והשיגוך

ארור אתה בעיר ... אתה בשדה ארור

טנאך ומשארתך א... ...נך ופרי אדמתך

שגר אלפיך וע... ...רור אתה בבאר

וארור אתה בצא... יהוה בך את המארה

את המהומה ואת ... ...רת בכל משלח ידך

אשר תעשה ... ...ר עד אבדך מהר

מפני רע ידבק יהוה בך ...

את הדבר עד כלתו ... מעל האדמה אשר

אתה בא שמה לרי... יככה יהוה בשחפת

ובקדחת ובדלקת ה... ...ר ובחרב ובשדפון

ובירקון ורדפוך עד ... והיו שמיך אשר על

ראשך נחשת והארץ ... תחתיך ברזל יתן

יהוה את מטר ארצך ...עפר מן השמים ירד

עליך עד השמדך י... ...וה נגף לפני איביך

בדרך אחד תצא א... ...שבעה דרכים תנוס

לפניו והיית לזעוה ... ...לכות הארץ והיתה

נבלתך למאכל לכ... ...מים ולבהמת הארץ

ואין מחריד יככ... ...ין מצרים ובעפלים

ובגרב ובחרס ... ...כל להרפא יככה

יהוה בשגעון ... ...ון לבב והיית

ממשש בצה... ...עור באפלה

ולא תצליח א... עשוק וגזול

B-14529

Our bondage sets us free.

There is a commandment given to the Jewish people, which is meant to provide a physical manifestation of the bondage that a free man accepts upon himself. *Tefillin* are bound to the arm and head as a sign of subservience to God.

In the Holocaust many were given an additional sign. The numbers B-14529 were tattooed on my father's left forearm at the death camp, Auschwitz-Birkenau.

Our bondage to God is remembered with a binding upon the arm. While our near-extinction by the Nazis is commemorated with a branding upon the very same arm.

Beneath our God-given sign of the *tefillin*, the Nazis provided my father with a new sign. This doubly marked arm stands as a clear emblem of our devotion to God. Whether we are being freed from bondage or burned in ovens, our faith does not waiver.

When people asked the Satmar Rav for a blessing, he would instruct the seeker to find a person with death camp numbers under his *tefillin*. There, he said, he would find a suitable person to convey blessings.

(Commentary continues in Book Two on page 107)

Bound

One of the wonderful things about exploration through art is the way the process evolves.

I begin with a concept, but I remain open to influence. I believe the greatest creative component is the creative process.

I don't think a single piece in this collectionended up looking like what my mind's eye had envisioned from the start.

In this piece, I had no intention of showing the Divine influence. It was strictly a piece in praise of God's people. But to my pleasant surprise, I ended up understanding that while God's people did miraculously hold it all together, their God never really let go.

The
survivors
not only
survived
...they were
saved.

It is very easy to lose sight of our uniqueness; to ignore our semblance to the image of God and wipe out any chance we have of relating to the Creator. The vast expanse of utterly empty space stretching billions of light-years in every direction taunts us, belittles us and defeats us. Therefore a reminder of our true exalted state is necessary.

When we bless the wine, we proclaim God as the creator of the fruit-of-the-vine. But we are not eating the fruit-of-the-vine. We are drinking the squeezed, refined, and fermented *juice* of the fruit-of-the-vine. For the wine we do not proclaim God as the creator. God's creation ended with the grape. It is man who takes God's grape and creates the wine. By praising God for His part, we are acknowledging a portion that is our part. The blessing over wine affirms our unique status as co-creators.

Only as fellow creators can we expect, and even demand, that God take notice of us. What's more, we can now take notice of God!

God is one, and man is one-of-a-kind.

(Commentary continues in Book Two on page 109)

L'Chayim

56

Primer II

"God created the Torah two thousand years before He created the universe".
(Midrash Beraishis Rabbah, 8)

"When the time came to create the universe, God used the Torah as a blueprint. Just as a builder places walls where the blueprint says to put them, and doors where the blueprint says to put them, God created the Torah and used that as a blueprint".
(Midrash Beraishis Rabbah 1:1)

To best understand the components of the equation set forth in the 'Primer I' on page 12,

$$G = g \neq e = G$$

(Where G stands for God, g for good, e for evil)

I delved deeply into the one document whose existence predates existence. As the blueprint for this universe, the Torah must account for, and possibly even provide an interpretation for, all we experience as reality. Somewhere in that blueprint there must be the specs for a Treblinka, a Mauthausen, and the rest of the concentration camps. Somewhere in plain view, there must be some variance, some legal dispensation, granting permission for such an aberration.

As the Torah must exist before the emergence of existence, so too what follows actually came first. The following essays chronicle my foray into, and in some cases out of, the abyss we call existence. They expose the dilemmas, highlight the conflicts, and ultimately reveal the inspirations which spawned the art found in *Book One*. Some of this art stands as monument; others are epitaph, but all represent a battleground where belief wars with unbelief, and horror with hope. In them all you will find an account of my efforts at uncovering the proper dimensions, perspectives and scale, employed by the Torah and reflected in its creation: the universe.

A Lasting Impression

The history of the relationship between humanity and God has been a long narrative of man's failures to live up to expectations. No one ever said humanity was perfect

Yet the book of Jonah relates to us that the people of Ninveh were worthy of compassion because of their inability to stand trial: "Shall I not take pity upon Ninveh the great city, in which there are more than a hundred and twenty thousand persons who do not know their right hand from their left?"[1]

If this is so, then what may the Jewish people say to God? We have more than stood trial; six million executions. This, I submit, has altered the case against the human race forever.

Are we, who have painfully learned the difference between our right and our left, not worthy of God's mercy? When the power to destroy a life is vested in the tip of a finger, the direction of a pointing, to the right: life, to the left: death, can any tribunal, on earth or in heaven, find probable cause beyond a reasonable doubt to convict us? In light of the immense darkness cast upon the earth by the Second World War, our post-Holocaust generations can not only stand trial, but can emerge victorious.

Humanity's brush with genocide has left it groping for the God it once knew. It reaches out, in an effort to embrace the Benevolent, the Miraculous, the Compassionate One. What it finds is Unfamiliar, Unforgiving, and by all human standards, Unfair. The embrace seems to constrict until almost all circulation has been cut off. The post-Holocaust encounter with the Divine confounds the senses and leaves man filled with existential angst and nihilistic nightmares.

There seems to exist a heavenly deception akin to the ruse played upon Isaac for the blessings. Isaac is confused when his son presents himself on the one hand sounding like Jacob and on the other feeling like Esau: "The voice is Jacob's voice, but the hands are Esau's hands".[2]

Esau's hands: the embodiment of brute force with their bony knuckles and chapped wrinkled-skin throbbing with a tangled network of pulsating veins that bulge through their wrists and up massive forearms, themselves covered in coarse, unruly hair, dangling and swaying from huge ape-like shoulders. It is these grotesque limbs which man must, not only contend, but embrace.

This divine duplicity finds expression in the song of *Ha'azinu*. God proclaims, "See, now, that I, I am He".[3] Normally such redundancy would not be tolerated in reference to God. It intimates that there is more than one God. This of course is not the intention, as we see the verse continue with, "...and no god is with Me."

Instead, it is explained in *Pirke D'Rebbi Eliezer*[4] that the first 'I' refers to God's interaction with the Jewish people during the exodus from Egypt, while the second one describes His involvement in the final redemption.

Rav Gedalya Schorr explains that God's identification of Himself as both an 'I' (first person) and an 'I' Who is a 'He' (third person), accounts for the disparity we have noticed in the behavior of the one and only: God.

In the last verse of Psalm 81 we find a similar mingling of grammatical form, "And while *He* would feed it with the fat of wheat, *I* would satisfy you with honey out of the rock". Both references are to God, yet the former is in third person while the latter is in first person.

Explains Rav Schorr, when God relates to us through blessings, He comes to us in the first person. Blessings are a form of interaction with God which mortal man can comprehend. Hence, God can appear in the first person as a direct cause and effect. When God must relate to man on a level perceived as curses, He is harder to understand and our relationship to Him becomes strained.

Our God is 'He', but we must never lose sight of the fact that 'He' is really 'I'. As the verse concludes in the first person, "... *I* put to death ... *I* strike down..." Faith demands that we recognize that while the hands are that of Esau, the voice is that of Jacob. The apparent stranglehold evil places upon humankind is no more than, "the skins of the goat-kids [with which] she covered [Jacob's] arms and his smooth-skinned neck."[5] The blessings and the curse, the voice and the hands, both emanate and belong to the one loving God.

It is modern man's ability to attend the masquerade party yet see past the masks of evil that guarantees him acquittal.

H i d e   &   S e e k

For an exquisite description of the human condition I must quote directly from the words of Rav Joseph B. Soloveitchik. He left us the most honest insights into the heart of one of Judaism's greatest minds. His eloquence in portraying the emotional angst and genuine separation anxiety inherent in man's distance from his Creator is unparalleled.

The Rav begins, "To be religious is not to be confused with living at ease, with unruffled calmness and inner peace. On the contrary, the religious life is fraught with emotional strife, intellectual tensions which ravel and fray its harmony. The religious experience not only warms, but also chills with horror. The religious is not only swayed by joy, but also by sadness and pain. All the modern theories about the healing function of religion see only one phase of the religious experience, the sublimated one. At the primeval stage, the experience is marked by the chill and rigor of the unknown. Only when man lives through the great encounter with the unknown in the night of doubt, suffering incessant dread and depression, does he experience the daybreak of a cheerful faith, full of promise of delivery and bliss. Moreover, in the very experience of doom and horror there is an undertone of joy. In the hopeless pain of surrender, in the tragedy of wrestling with the mysterious *ish* (the man who wrestled with Jacob in the night) the contours of a great and joyful drama of existence are discernable.[1]

Not always do the heavens proclaim the glory of God. Instead, man encounters a seemingly unresponsive attitude on the part of the cosmic forces towards man, his needs and his aspirations. Man feels a grisly emptiness and chilling cruelty pervading the uncharted lanes of the universe; encumbering, vast, almost endless distances suggest to man the stillness, darkness and insensation of Being which is intimately knit with non-being. Nature is cool, mechanical and devoid of meaning; man, searching for salvation, is a tragic-comical figure crying out to a mute insensible environment, which does not share his troubles and suffering.[2]

Many a time man wonders whether or not God cares to intervene on his behalf. The tragic search for God, Who hides His face, is the great undertaking of man, and it frequently ends in despair and resignation. The Torah abounds in the complaints and pleas of the prophets who, even as they were committed to God and had unshakable faith in Him, were frightened by His absence from their midst. They were terrified by thoughts of the void, the weird darkness and chaos preceding creation, and dismayed by prayers unheard, and sacrifices rejected, and martyrdom incurred seemingly in vain by the just and righteous. The prophet shudders, seeing a world ruled by inhumanity and brutality.[3]

The experience of the *numen absens*, of an empty world, at a cosmic and historical level, is shattering. And not only the stately joy of faith and closeness to the Infinite, but also the sadness and gloom of metaphysical solitude and existential void flow from a religious fountainhead. The experience of a deserted, dreary world must not be confused with agnosticism or Greek mythological fatalism. It is the religious emotion at its best. Solitary man, who reads the unknown and who feels lost in a boundless universe, does not fall prey to his fearful experiences, however distressing the latter might prove to be. He shows remarkable resilience. Therefore, he is not to be categorized by the ancient Greek tragedy, where human action is completely compulsive, where freedom of decision and initiative are absent, and man just a withered leaf carried along by a raging, absurd storm. In Judaism, the numinous experience is a prologue to redemption - man hopes to free himself finally from the dreadful, and to march forward towards beatitude and bliss. Eschatology is the final destination of the religious experience, and an eschatological experience means a redeemed one, when the now unknown will appear in our midst as an old friend and acquaintance, when man will see God, feel His presence, and enjoy Him continuously, when the curtain of the numinous will be raised.[4]

At this point we come face to face with another aspect of the human depth crisis-the loneliness of man in the universe. He is thrown into a world that has neither regard nor understanding for his singular role. He is a tiny speck, floating in a vast sea of brute thinghood and mechanical existence. The other intelligent Being in Whom he may find sympathy and concern is distant and invisible, hiding behind the cloud of mystery and transcendence. The numinous experience of God casts its shadow upon the surroundings of man. If God is absent from the immediate end, then man is trapped. When he lifts his eyes he sees only dreary spaces and emptiness. "A roaring sea moves toward him, darkness engulfs him". (Isaiah 5:30)[5]

Hence, the formation of accidental friendships at a finite level does not give comfort to a lonely soul. The craving for love must be gratified at the plane of the God-man encounter. Only through such a meeting, at which the finite creature addresses itself to the Creator, is an I - Thou relationship established, thus providing man with something that he could not attain in his social life, namely, the awareness of togetherness and community existence. The best medium through which such a paradoxical fellowship is achieved is the prayer-dialogue. In prayer, man tries to break through the unknown to the *kerygamatic* and to attain contact with the creator, to convert tenseness into intimacy, strangeness into acquaintance. Judaism wants him to take courage and address himself to God, and by boldly approaching Him-the Infallible and Unknowable-to lift the veil and dreadful mystery of the *numen*. When this takes place, man finds the unknown to be an old friend; in the *numen* he discovers the intimately Unknown, radiating warmth and love. Through prayer, man accomplishes the impossible: the transformation of the numinous into the *kerygamatic*, of fear into love and of absence into presence. Thus when prayer is born, a community is established and man finds himself no longer lonely, forlorn; there are two lonely beings who have sought and found each other".[6]

- Rav Joseph B. Soloveitchik -

As the Rav eloquently relates to us, all this cat-and-mouse, hide-and-seek of the religious experience serves a purpose beyond frustration and despair. For post-Holocaustic generations, however, the experience of the *numen absens* has taken on an opacity of blinding proportions.

The hidden nature of the Holocaust is a major component of its make-up. When the extermination of Jews first began, the numbers of deaths being reported were so outlandish that they were met with skepticism. As the war raged on the horror remained a well-kept secret. By the time liberators reached the camps, much of the hard evidence had been destroyed. But most incredible

of all is the emergence of outright Holocaust deniers. Even while the victims still roam the planet, there are those who deny their stories.

But it is not only the existence of Holocaust deniers that work to hide the Holocaust from view. The lack of a serious response to the nearly total eclipse of understanding brought on by the Holocaust has only served to bury the beast even deeper. Refusing to even attempt to bring the Holocaust under some context of faith is tantamount to denying its existence altogether. Professed believers approach the Holocaust with extreme reserve. They limit their involvement to tales of rescue and divine salvation. They ignore the fact that divine intervention cuts both ways, and the side facing us at this time is divine damnation, not salvation. By allowing ourselves the comfort of focusing on the meager 'bright spots', we cast an ever darkening shadow upon the real message of the Holocaust.

It is precisely the hidden nature of the Holocaust that provides the strongest indication that there is much to learn from this particular cataclysm. Reb Yehudah Aryeh Leib Alter, better known as the Sfas Emes, uncovers a secret about secrets. He says that the more something is hidden, the more holiness it contains. Buried beneath the rubble of the darkest destruction lies the potential for the greatest blessing. As the legend goes, the Messiah will share his birthday with the anniversary of the destruction of both Holy Temples!

The Sfas Emes illustrates his point with the famous dream of Pharaoh.[7] When Pharaoh has his dream foretelling the economic future of Egypt and the rest of the world, he sees seven fat, healthy cows rising out of the Nile, followed by seven emaciated, sickly cows. The scrawny cows open their mouths wide and swallow their engorged counterparts — a bizarre sight, certainly. But what really startles Pharaoh is the fact that while the skinny cows gorged themselves on the fat cows, their feast left them none the plumper. The consumption left absolutely no sign of the fat, healthy cows whatsoever.

This, says the Sfas Emes, represents the nature of the dark exile we find ourselves in. There may not be any sign of hope or deliverance, but precisely within the veil of darkness exists the seeds of salvation. Within those bovine skeletons lay the healthy cows, which represented seven years of blessing. Without the cursed years, the full blessing of the first seven years would not have made such an impact. The blessing truly existed within the cursed.

Therefore, while the Holocaust would seem to be the most unlikely place to find faith, it just might be the best place to look.

Turn the Page

Our view of God is clearly obscured. His beneficent ways are shrouded in mystery and veiled in secrecy. The light of God's presence no longer shines warm and bright. In its place we must bear a cold and dark, almost blank, stare. A man could go blind trying to catch a glimpse of the God he has fallen in love with. Try as he may, the world around him presents him with very little evidence that his beloved still cares. In light of all this darkness, Rav Soloveitchik resorts to prayer, "The best medium through which such a paradoxical fellowship is achieved is the prayer-dialogue. In prayer, man tries to break through the unknown to the *kerygamatic* and to attain contact with the Creator".[1]

Can we, however, really expect our voices to pick up where our sight has left off? Doesn't the Talmud tell us in the name of R. Eleazar that, "From the day on which the Temple was destroyed the gates of prayer have been closed"?[2]

To make matters worse, with the destruction of the temple and its services, we lost not only our voices, but our manual dexterity. We no longer had the strength to offer sacrifices as a form of communication with God.

All this leaves us with a Jewish nation that is badly crippled. Its eyesight is weak, its vocal cords severed, and it limps along in practically full paralysis. Therefore R. Eleazar accurately captures the Jewish nation's condition when he proclaims that only one gate is open to supplication. "Though the gates of prayer are closed the gates of weeping are not closed".[3]

The only currency we have left are the tears that well up in our eyes. Unfortunately, tears are a commodity we have in abundance. But what is it about tears that provide them exclusive rights to the inner sanctum?

The Maharal explains that the Temple represented the life force in the world. With the loss of this life force all modes of experience of a forceful, energetic, or powerful nature were rendered impotent. Tears sneak past all the closed gates because they stem from man's humble, beaten, and contrite nature.

The Talmud[4] explores the prayer of Hannah in its quest to understand the various aspects of proper prayer. It is widely accepted that her style of prayer is worthy of emulation. Even a superficial overview of her approach will make it clear to us how different our communicative position vis-à-vis the Creator is from earlier times.

Hannah was barren, and she was one of two wives of Elkanah. The other wife was Penina who mothered many children. In an attempt to get Hannah to pray fervently for a child, Penina taunted Hannah with sharp words. Although Penina had good intentions, she was punished for her verbal abuse.

Hannah's prayer is quoted in the Talmud as follows, "If Thou wilt *look* [give me a child] it is well, and if Thou wilt not *look*, I will go and seclude myself with a man who is not my husband, with the full knowledge of my husband, Elkanah, and as I shall have been alone [with another man] they will make me drink the water of the suspected wife, and they cannot falsify Your Law, which says, '[An innocent woman who drinks the waters of suspicion] she shall be cleared and shall conceive seed!'"

Hannah's prayer takes on a confrontational tone — an ultimatum of sorts. Instead of contrition, Hannah offers threats. She is undaunted by God's omnipotence, but not unaware of it. Hannah is the first person to call God the 'Lord of Hosts'. Hannah's approach is not due to a lack of respect. It is due to a full appreciation of the relationship God wants with his people. He wants to see passion in our pleas. He wants to hear resolve in our prayers. And He wants us to fight, even against Him, for our cause.

It is these talents that have been lost since the destruction. What is not clear is if the present condition is a result of the gates being closed, or if the gates have closed due to our lack of approach. Must tears flow until the Temple returns, or is the Temple waiting for us to stop crying?

Broken Glass

Our descent into the Holocaustic abyss begins on a pair of cold November nights in 1938. The mass destruction of that event may be unique, but the symbolism has been a part of Jewish lore since the time of the Talmud.[1]

As the wedding guests worked themselves into a joyous frenzy, celebrating the union of another young Jewish couple, a sudden panic filled the dance hall. The spine chilling crackle of shattered glass quieted the revelers. The source of the disruption came from the head table. There, the father of the groom had taken hold of a precious glass goblet; instead of the usual toast he opted to loosen his grip and allow the valuable vessel to plummet to the ground and shatter into countless shards.[2]

This historic 'anti-toast', from the fourth century, soon becomes immortalized and incorporated into the standard Jewish wedding ceremony.[3] The adopted custom dictates that before the bride and groom leave the wedding canopy, the groom lowers his foot with a defiant, almost victorious gesture, and breaks a fine crystal glass.

As the groom and his bride join forces and prepare to build a family, their initial step meets with disaster. Their union treads upon dangerous slivers and they are forced to sidestep the now useless shards. They have joined in order to build, yet their first movement destroys.

The origins of the 'broken glass' may date back to the fourth century, however, our generation is painfully aware that glass does not just break under the wedding canopy. On November 9th, 1938 the Holocaust begins with *Kristallnacht* (Crystal Night), a reference to the untold numbers of broken windows of synagogues, Jewish-owned stores, community centers, and homes plundered and destroyed during vicious riots encouraged by the Nazi regime.

Amidst all the panes of glass that have come crashing down upon the Jewish people, how is it that the sound of a single glass broken under the wedding canopy can still be heard? Where do we get the courage to rebuild, remarry, and rejoice? Could the deliberate glass-breaking at a wedding help us cope with the belligerent night of glass breaking in the streets of Germany?

The Maharsha, a commentator on the Talmud, analyzes the origins of this strange custom. The secret, he feels, lies in the material itself. According to the Maharsha, glass is analogous to the fragility of a man's life. Glass is made of grains of sand, and when it shatters into tiny pieces, it can no longer be repaired. So too, man is made of dust and when he dies, he returns to dust. The glass represents the fragility and temporality of a man's life. The message being driven home is that life is fleeting. It will come to an end as it began. A man's life, and all he achieves, will one day vanish without a trace.

If that is the point, why not use a ceramic vessel instead of glass? Ceramics are produced from earth (exactly like man) and are equally irreparable when broken. The answer may lie in the fact that glass is ultimately recyclable, where ceramics are not. A glass vessel cannot be mended, but a new vessel can be constructed from the remains. Ceramics, on the other hand, are lost forever. Man's life is more similar to glass; it will come to an end, but his existence will endure.

But what does all this have to do with the joy of a wedding day? Human mortality is one thing, and celebrating life's special occasions is quite another. Doesn't *Koheles* say that there is "A time to weep, and a time to laugh; a time to mourn, and a time to dance"?[4] Why must we dampen our spirits at a wedding of all places?

To fully understand the decision to shatter our spirits at a wedding, we must look at yet another incident,[5] which no doubt ranks as the most outlandish expression of despair. At the wedding of the fourth-century Babylonian *Amora* Mar Bar Ravina, the Rabbis ask Rav Hamnuna Zuta to sing a song in celebration of this joyous event. He obliged by chanted to them, "Alas for us that we are to die! Alas for us that we are to die!" Unsure of the meaning behind these words, Rav Hamnuna Zuta's disciples ask him what chorus should accompany his mournful ballad; he tells them to respond with Torah and good deeds. In other words, do not allow yourselves to sink into depression, but spring into action. What we have then is not a rally cry in support of nihilism, but quite the opposite. It is an attempt to focus our attention on loftier realities, which ultimately bring us to greater degrees of joy

The Talmud relates an even clearer expression of our idea in the following tale:[6] When R. Eliazer ben Azariah was asked to head up the academy, he asked his wife if he should accept the position. She said to him: "Perhaps they will depose you later on". He replied to her: "[There is a proverb] Let a man use a cup of distinction for even one day even if it be broken the next".

Here too we see that a recognition of the transient nature of this world should not deter us from enjoying the brief existence we are privileged to have.

Breaking the glass is not meant to spoil the party, rather, it provides us with the necessary perspective. We should not make the mistake of rejoicing as if there is anything intrinsically worthwhile. All this will soon end. King David makes this point by contrasting the desire of the masses to fix their pleasure in this world on tangible success, "O that we would be shown some good!"[7] while for David himself, "Thou hast already put joy in my heart, more than when their grain and their wine increase".[8] His joy is not dependent on external conditions, which will ultimately vanish with the passing time. The masses wait for an increase in their grain and wine to find an excuse to rejoice, while King David experiences the kind of joy that transcends time and space. Go ahead, be brave enough to use a cup of distinction, a cup that was made exceptionally ornate, regardless of its fleeting nature.

The colloquial phrase; "eat, drink, be merry ... for tomorrow we die", is often attributed to defining a hedonistic outlook, but it actually comes from *Kohellet* 8:15: "Then I commended mirth, because a man hath no better thing under the sun than to eat, and to drink, and to be merry: for that shall abide with him of his labour the days of his life, which God giveth him under the sun". If we are mindful of our numbered days under the sun, and we still do not refrain from living a full life, then our merriment will be appropriate.

We find an interesting example of misguided joy from none other than Job. In Chapter 29 verse 18 Job laments his distorted view on life. "And I said, I will perish with my nest, and I will multiply days as the Phoenix". Job lived life as if he were the mythical bird, the Phoenix. A bird which has the ability to live forever. As Job says, it perishes with its nest, but never fails to rise from the ashes, to live on. Job ignored his own mortality. All his joys in life were obtained by instilling a false intrinsic and eternal value to his possessions and achievements.

The *Midrash*[9] acknowledges the existence of this eternal bird in two conflicting *Midrashim*. The first one encounters the Phoenix in the Garden of Eden. It is the only animal not to partake of the Tree of Knowledge, hence it lives forever. In another *Midrash*[10] we find the Phoenix aboard Noah's ark where he is blessed by Noah with eternal life for not placing any demands upon Noah. All the other animals required very specific diets and feeding schedules, while the Phoenix sat in the corner minding his own business. The conflict is apparent, if the Phoenix did not eat from the Tree of Knowledge, and he was immortal, there was no reason to expel him from the Garden of Eden. (God explicitly tells us that man was expelled because he ate from the Tree of Knowledge lest he now eat from the Tree of Life and live forever). Furthermore, if he already had immortality what was the use in Noah's blessing?

There also exists two opinions as to the life cycle of the Phoenix. The school of Rav Yannai maintained: The Phoenix lives a thousand years. At the end of a thousand years, a fire issues from its nest and burns it up, yet of the bird a piece the size of an egg is left; it grows new limbs and lives again. However, Rav Yuman son of Rav Simeon said: At the end of a thousand years. Its body dries up and its wings drop off. Yet of the bird a piece the size of an egg is left; it grows new limbs and lives again.

I'd like to reconcile these opinions by proposing the possibility of two Phoenix birds. One belonging to our temporal existence on the outskirts of Eden, and one reserved for the world that was meant to be before the fall. Convenient to my theory, the Phoenix is referred to by two different names. In Job, it is called the *Chul*, while the one aboard the ark is referred to as the *Urshaina*.

The *Chul* is described by the school of Rav Yannai as having no deterioration. It simply is consumed by its nest and reborn. This bird doesn't really die in as much as it simply evolves. At all stages of its life it experiences no obstacles, no ills, no effects of time whatsoever. For the *Chul* his death appears out of nowhere. He never sees it coming. His days are lived in full strength and without the slightest sign that it will ever end — a phenomenon completely foreign to our world.

The *Urshaina* belongs to this world. That is why it was found on the Ark. As described by Rav Yudan, this bird feels the effects of time and his body experiences the aging process. His death is continual and can be felt with each progressing day. The *Urshaina* may live forever, but his life, like ours, is one of continual dying. Of him it can be said that he has the day of his death in his sights.

Originally, even post-Eden man lived like the *Chul*. He lived out his years without deterioration until one day he sneezed and gave up his soul. It was Abraham who prayed that this should not be the way of man. He prayed that the human body should deteriorate day by day. Why? So man would be cognizant of his mortality and repent from his evil ways. Abraham realized the importance of being ever mindful that our mortality will, sooner or later, render all our actions useless, and therefore we must focus on the only path to the everlasting: that of repentance. Do not live as if there is any intrinsic worth to our fleeting actions. With every passing moment, be fully aware of its utter transience. We must shatter the glass which is blown from none other than... *chul* (sand).

Breaking the glass is meant to sober us up without bringing us to despair. Man must develop an attitude towards life where he can experience death on a daily basis, and find a way to live through it. We are compared to the *Urshaina*; we meet defeat with a renewed vigor and ultimately rise from the ashes. The human spirit is ultimately recyclable.

KIDDUSH LEVANA

Marriage is the epitome of rebirth. It must be embarked upon with this frame of mind. Yes, all this couple will build will ultimately vanish from the face of the earth, and we will still rejoice in their union, because that is what the Creator wants from his creations. Celebration from this perspective is of the highest order. When it is superficial and found as merely a natural reaction to a situation, it is ill founded and inappropriate.

Allow me an analogy or two from nature itself. Take for example, the mighty waves of the ocean. The verse in Isaiah, "The wicked are like the troubled sea",[11] is explained by the *Midrash*[12] as a metaphor for the way the wicked ignore their ultimate fate. They are able to exalt themselves as they rise, though each of them is shattered when it reaches the sand, and must retreat back to the sea. The *Midrash* goes on to describe the malady of the wicked in exactly the same terms we have mentioned concerning the message of the breaking glass: "Even though each successive wave sees the proceeding shattered, it too exalts itself as it rises and will not return to the sea! So it is with the wicked. Though they see what happen to the others, still they exalt themselves".

Should we then not rejoice at all? Is our ability to rejoice in the face of the impending sandy beach, folly? As we have said, if we celebrate in spite of the sand that lies ahead rather than ignoring it, then it is praiseworthy.

We find in the Talmud[13] that when King Herod

wanted to plait the marble walls of the temple in gold, the Rabbis prohibited him from doing so. They preferred the wavy pattern found in the veins of the stone. Its appearance resembled the ocean waves! Rav Hutner understands the metaphor of the waves exactly the way we have been learning throughout this essay. The Temple was close to being destroyed by the Romans, and the Rabbis feared that the people would begin to give up on the Temple service, feeling it was a futile exercise. The waves showed the people that in spite of certain defeat, the wave summons all its strength and raises itself up in a posture of defiance and determination.

The wave behaves the same way every time, yet its actions can be compared to the wicked and the saintly alike. The difference lies in the motivation and intent. King David doesn't shy away from learning how to behave from the actions of the wicked, "In order to bring the deeds of men to follow the word of Thy lips, I observe the paths of the lawbreakers".[14] Since the wicked are driven by their desires, and fail to see the utter futility of their ways, often their actions are performed with ingenuity and a hearty dose of adrenaline. The righteous, who are burdened with foresight, must emulate the passion for life of the wicked, and live with an equal amount of gusto and bravado.

From the waves of the ocean we now turn to the phases of the moon. There is a blessing recited over the waxing moon every month. It celebrates the moon's renewal and rebirth and implores the moon to accept its fate with joy and gladness. It is a crown of splendor for the Jewish people who are destined to renew themselves in a similar fashion. In consonance with all we have been saying, it's no wonder that this prayer is associated with great joy. The blessing is said only at times when extreme expression of joy is appropriate. No mention is made

about the impending waning. It is irrelevant. So important is this concept that Rabbi Yochanan taught that one who sanctifies the new moon is as if he welcomed the *Shechina* itself.[15] It is so vital to the survival of the Jewish people that God makes this blessing of the moon their very first commandment. Even before the giving of the Torah and before leaving Egypt, the Jewish people must be able to celebrate the waxing in spite of the impending waning.

This is exactly why the prophet Isaiah admonished King Hezekiah. "And Isaiah … came to him [King Hezekiah] and said, '… You shall die, and not live'".[16] 'You shall die' in this world, and 'You will not live' in the next world. When Hezekiah asked him, "Why a punishment so severe?" Isaiah replied, "Because you did not try to have children". And Hezekiah replied, "I did not because it was shown to me by the Holy Spirit that children coming from me will not be worthy". To that Isaiah said, "What have you to do with the secrets of God? What you have been commanded, you should have done, and let God do what He pleases".[17]

During the Holocaust, there were plenty of reasons to give up on life. To abandon the religion, to forsake, and to deny. Yet we hear numerous accounts depicting phoenix-like rejuvenative powers. The gall of a people who could celebrate a wedding in the midst of the Warsaw Ghetto. Or a people who could huddle in a corner of a concentration camp barrack and ignite a *Chanukiah* in celebration of Chanukah. And not just light, but recite: "Blessed are You, *HaShem* our God, King of the universe, Who has kept us alive, sustained us, and brought us to this time". And brought us to this time?! This time of horror and annihilation?! Yes! To this time; especially this time. A time where we will witness a nation of believers beyond belief.

Destination Unknown

The Ramban[1] teaches us that, whatever happened to the Patriarchs is a portent for their descendants. We can therefore find many similarities between the life and times of the biblical characters and ourselves.

One such connection can be drawn from Abraham's relocation to the Holy Land. When God instructs Abraham to leave his homeland, He specifically leaves out a very important detail. God neglects to tell him where he is to go. Instead, God assures him that he will eventually show him his destination, but for now, he must focus on leaving rather than arriving.

Rav Yerucham, in the work titled, *Daas Torah*[2] makes a striking insight into the mechanics of God's ways. He says that if God had told Abraham where He was leading

him, the entire journey would have been reduced to a single commandment. His travels would have been in preparation of fulfilling the commandment of relocating to Canaan. Had he never arrived in Canaan, it follows that he would have neglected to perform God's will.

By hiding the destination from Abraham, God allowed him to focus his service on the task at hand. From the moment Abraham set out on his journey, he was credited with fulfilling God's commandment in its entirety. Instead of a single commandment, Abraham enjoyed fulfillment with each and every step he took. Each step becomes a *Mitzvah*.

This transformation is more than a simple transference from the whole to its parts. By withholding vital information from Abraham, God actually heightened the amount of internal struggle required to perform God's will. Abraham was not provided the luxury of setting his sights on the goal of his actions. Instead, he was forced to put all his energies into his actions on the merit of faith and faith alone. In this way, the sum of the parts became exponentially greater than the whole.

Dr. Victor Frankl is famous for postulating that man is constantly in search of meaning. As a psychologist who witnessed firsthand the horrors of World-War II from within the confines of a concentration camp, he testified to the fact that survival often depended upon the inmate's ability to infuse meaning into his nightmare. Void of meaning, man will contemplate suicide even under idyllic life circumstances; full of meaning, man will endure even the death camps of the Nazi regime.

By stripping Abraham of a destination, God robbed him of all meaning. Faith became his only straw to grasp. Abraham had to face the great unknown armed with only a desire to fulfill the will of God.

We might try and dismiss Abraham's great faith as a trivial matter. After all, his orders came directly from the Almighty. Not only that, but God promised Abraham that He would make him a great nation, and bless him above all others. Is there really much of a leap of faith in following a divine directive?

I would suggest there is. First, it is a mistake to equate perceived good with divine action. The same God that we assume will protect Abraham and lead him to a tranquil land, herded Abraham's children onto cattle cars and transported them to gas chambers and crematoria. Secondly, as it turned out for Abraham himself, the land of Canaan, the 'final destination', started out looking more like the 'final solution'. Abraham arrived amidst a dreadful famine. He was forced to leave and seek sustenance from Egypt. While in Egypt, his life was put in danger, and Pharaoh kidnapped his wife, Sarah. As it turned out, the great unknown, even if led there by God Himself, was still a death-defying hike rather than a walk in the park.

We can now compare Abraham's exodus from his homeland to that of his descendants' deportation from theirs. As Abraham travelled aimlessly in search of a homeland, his children would eventually board trains completely unaware of the duration of their trip, let alone their final destination. Initially the deportees must have assumed that a trip of only a few hours could possibly lie ahead. After all, they were packed into the cattle cars shoulder to shoulder without room to even sit down, and with no facilities whatsoever. So when the 'click-clack' of the railway track kept its monotonous pace beyond the initial few hours, they became afflicted by every 'click' and every 'clack' of the endless track of rail.

In Abraham's case, he was rewarded step by step. In the case of European Jewry, they were credited for enduring every jolt, every jostle, every hum, and every screech along the way.

However we understand, or fail to understand, the Holocaust, the experience felt by the victims of the war had a purpose. Obviously, the purpose was not of an apparent positive nature, and the fact that God hid their destination from them allowed for the fulfillment of God's will at every stage of the trip. God counted every agonizing minute as its own mini Holocaust.

This concept of breaking things up into bite-sized pieces is found in a number of circumstances. For instance, when the Jews sinned with the Golden Calf, God is eventually appeased by Moses' pleas, and forgives the people, but their act is not forgotten, and a price has to be paid. If God would have exacted punishment from the people in one lump sum, they would have perished. Instead He dissipated the punishment down through centuries of pogroms, crusades and expulsions. As R. Isaac said: "No retribution comes upon the world without its fraction of retribution for the sin of the first calf".[3]

Indeed, it is hard to imagine a Holocaust of greater severity than the one we witnessed, but in some way every 'click and clack' along the path served to dissipate and test their resolve bit by bit before they even arrived at the death camps. By withholding information from the victims, a significant debt had been paid before ever reaching the camps.

In many ways life itself is a similar ordeal. Our final destination, *Olam HaBah*: the World to Come, is never even mentioned in the Torah, and no man knows the length of his days. In this way we live out our existence with an emphasis on the journey instead of the destination. Our accomplishments mount with every passing moment. Our time on this earth does not amount to a single life lived, but a myriad of moments experienced, moments squandered or cherished, wasted or enshrined for all time. We have the ability to transform the ephemeral, fleeting moments into everlasting achievements.

This is the lesson, Abraham learned on his journey from *Haran* — the Jews on their way to the camps. Each step, each railroad tie, stood out as a unit. There was no blurring of time into hours, days, or weeks. Each moment was felt and lived through on its own merit.

The Torah portion in which the Jewish people are labeled a holy nation[4] describes the importance of focusing on the task at hand. There, it describes a transgression in the sacrificial service based exclusively on a misdirection of thought. '*Pigul*' arises from a disconnect between one's actions and one's thoughts. Perfect performance and adherence to all details of the service are not enough. If a person has a different goal in mind while performing the service, that thought renders the service invalid.

There is a tendency to allow ourselves to be lulled into a monotonous existence where each act resembles the last and is indistinguishable from the next. What we need to do is let go of the destination, and embrace the journey.

Confine, Refine, Define

Unfortunately, the journey of the Eastern European Jews was one they'd sooner forget than embrace. In those cattle cars, the Jewish people were packed like the proverbial sardine: compressed to standing room only conditions for days and sometimes weeks on end. One can hardly avoid the comparison to the winepress of which King David refers in a number of his Psalms.

In the eighth Psalm, King David opens with a reference to what some believe is a musical instrument: the *gittis*.[1] However, Rav Samson Raphael Hirsch believes that *gittis* actually means a wine press. The wine press is a somewhat ghastly, torturous device used to crush the delicate fruit of the vine, and thereby forcibly extract its sweet nectar. From there the juice can ferment and become quite literally 'nectar of the gods'. Wine has an exalted place in almost all societies, and when King David conjures up the wine-making process as the theme for this Psalm, he has a very specific agenda in mind.

To fully understand King David's intent, and how it relates to man's development, we must begin at the beginning...

The Torah does not tell us what type of fruit Adam and Eve ate in the Garden of Eden. However, the Talmud postulates on the matter, and according to Rav Meir, the Tree of Knowledge in the Garden of Eden was in fact not a tree, but a vine, and they didn't eat from it, rather they drank![2] The Talmud says[3] that, "The type of tree from which Adam ate was a grapevine; for there is nothing that brings as much wailing upon man as wine". The *Midrash* goes on to describe that Eve squeezed grapes and presented her husband with a goblet of wine.[4]

The crafty snake, and Eve's own ambition, enticed her to transgress God's only prohibition. She partook of the vine and shared it with her husband. The transformation was instantaneous as they immediately

realized they were naked. The sudden awareness of their nakedness was a clear signal that they now possessed the ability, or the need, to differentiate good from evil. The *good* spoken of, can be understood as *good* from a utilitarian point of view. Before their intoxication, the focus of their bodies was function, not form. Their actions had consequences, not implications.

The 19th Century German philosopher Arthur Schopenhauer describes the existence of a primal *Will*, which is the way man can relate to the world in its essence. Separate from this *Will*, he insists that man's intellect and reason function on a lower level by shaping and interpreting his view of the empirical world at large. It was this lower level, which Schopenhauer calls *representation*, that Eve found so attractive about the forbidden fruit. The Torah tells us that it was the *representation* of the fruit, as perceived by her senses, that enticed Eve, as it says, "And the woman perceived that the tree was good for eating and that it was a delight to the eyes and that the tree was desirable as a means to wisdom".[5]

While guided only by their God-given *Will*, Adam and Eve viewed their bodies as a means to an end. There was no *good* or *evil* inherent in their physical manifestation, any more than there is *good* or *evil* in a hammer or an axe. Once the *knowledge* or *representative force*, as Schopenhauer would call it, entered their consciousness, through their transgression, they no longer could function as pure *Will*. The world around them was now a complicated mix of *Will* and *representation*, and their bodies were ground zero in the battle.

Schopenhauer explains that the body is unique among all objects in the empirical world, because of its proximity to the self. It is the only entity that exists as both subject (Will) and object (representation). The French philosopher, Jean-Paul Sartre, following the likes of Descartes and Plato, conceived of polar realities he called 'Being and Nothingness'. These are synonymous with the human body being both an object (being) and a subject (nothingness). The Malbim, a

19th Century commentator, puts a metaphysical spin on this union by describing the soul as being separate from the body until the transgression, whereby the soul and body became one.

Having ingested the 'self-consciousness' enabling fruit, man dramatically shifted the mode of reality he was forever to inhabit. Adam and Eve immediately recognized their nakedness and sought to clothe themselves. Having covered themselves in foliage, they were suddenly gripped by a sense of dread and fear. As it says, "I heard the sound of You, [God] in the garden, and I was afraid because I am naked, so I hid". There would seem to be a disconnect between the cause and effect inherent in this verse. First of all, they were no longer naked. Secondly, if the source of their fear was their nakedness, the emotion should have been embarrassment, not fear. And if Adam really meant to refer to his sin, then why mention the manifestation of the sin rather than the sin itself?

Instead, I take this encounter as a preview of man's new-found mortality. As God promised, "... for on the day you eat of it, you shall surely die".[6] Adam and Eve where frightened because they were now capable of being conscious of their bodies as objects, which meant that they had entered an existence bound by space and time. Objectification of the self can occur only in a temporal structure. The most famous example of this phenomenon is provided by Edmund Husserl. He contends that, "When I experience a melody, I don't simply experience a knife-edge presentation (primal impression) of one note which is then completely washed away and replaced with the next knife-edge presentation of the next note. Rather, consciousness retains the sense of the first note as I hear the second note, a hearing that is also enriched by an anticipation (protention) of the next note (or at least, in case I do not know the melody, of the fact that there will be a next note, or some next auditory event)".[7]

When the verse stresses that the sound of God's voice could be heard travelling through the garden,[8] this is in line with Husserl's melody analogy. Adam had never 'heard' the voice of God before, although he had spoken with God, because the act of hearing requires a past, present, and future frame of reference. This auditory experience was indeed frightening for Adam and Eve. Furthermore, the reference to the sound moving through the garden solidifies man's spacial confines. Until this point, space and time were foreign concepts. This is in line with Immanuel Kant's doctrine of Transcendental Idealism. Kant's doctrine states that space and time are forms of human intuition, and they can only be proved valid for things as they appear to us and not for things as they are in themselves. There is clear and obvious evidence of the absence of spacial rules, as we perceive them, prior to the sin. While the Tree of Knowledge occupies center stage, figuratively and literally, having taken root at the absolute center of the garden, there is another tree, less spoken of, but no less important. "God made grow every tree that was pleasing to the sight and good for food, with the Tree of Life in the middle of the garden".[9] Both the Tree of Knowledge and the Tree of Life occupied the same central location at the same time. This phenomenon is sanctioned by Kantian doctrine, so long as the empirical world we experience is not objectified. Once it is, all the laws of space, time, and causality come rushing in to help us make sense of the experiences we observe.

As such, both trees play a vital role in our understanding of just how far Adam and Eve fell as a result of their transgression. While the Tree of Knowledge awakened man's self-consciousness, the Tree of Life was to grant immortality. Now if Adam and Eve were, indeed, beyond the confines of space, time, and causality, what use would the Tree of Life provide before the ingestion of the forbidden fruit of the Tree of Knowledge? It may not have held any real import at all. In fact, the Kli Yakir holds that the Tree of Life bore no fruit! So perhaps its sole purpose was to serve as a foil to our Tree of Knowledge, and teach us that by choosing the Tree of Knowledge they turned their back on immortality. It had no fruit, because it represented the status quo. Yet when the fruit of the Tree of Knowledge is imbibed, and humanity has fallen into the grips of mortal life, God expresses concern that man would now take from the Tree of Life and live forever. As it says, "lest he [man] put forth his hand and take also of the Tree of Life, and eat and live forever".[10] To insure that the Tree of Life is not violated, God places a fiery angel bearing a revolving sword in the path of any seeker. Why such concern for a barren tree, and why only now?

When God created the trees on the third day, He commanded them to bring forth fruit of their kind, meaning that the tree itself should taste like the fruit it bears. The *Midrash* tells us that the earth was concerned that if the bark tasted as good as the fruit, man would consume the tree and leave no source for the production of delicious fruit. So the earth rebelled and brought forth trees which produced fruit, but not of its kind. There was one tree, however, that did comply. The Tree of Life was delicious from bark to branch.

So the tree was edible, but why was it no longer on the menu? Why must a man's life eventually come to an end now that he has acquired the knowledge between

good and evil? It is true that our protagonists were warned: tasting the forbidden fruit would be fatal, however, this death sentence seems to be a consequence rather than a punishment. Since death is only a consequence, the Tree of Life retained the power to suspend mortality and grant eternal life. Had it been a punishment, no manner of action could annul it. The Tree of Life's *fountain of youth* would have dried up in the same way as the earth now could only bring forth thorns and thistles.

The Malbim, Rabbi Meir Leibush, raises a valid objection to the existence of a Tree of Life altogether. He contends that eternal life in this world is not a blessing but a curse. With all the suffering man must endure, what benefit would there be in living a life of pain and suffering in perpetuity? If this is the case, then why plant a Tree of Life altogether?

In order to reconcile the situation, the Malbim recognizes the distinction we made concerning life prior to the sin and life after the sin. It is only post-sin that the human condition turned unfavorable for immortality. Once man had allowed himself to become a mere object, life was no longer hospitable. As we see in God's punishment of man, "... through suffering shall you eat of it all the days of your life".[11] Life took on the characteristics of the wine press after Adam and Eve ate from the tree. And life lived in the *gittis* can only find respite in the grave.

This is why the path back to the Tree of Life is blocked after the sin. The Malbim understands that God does not wish to withhold good from His creations, and as such, allowed

the tree to pre-sin man and would not have wanted to block the way back to the Tree of Life for post-sin man were it not harmful to him.

The following story found in the Talmud[12] illustrates our position. At one point in his travels, Alexander the Great comes upon the gates of Eden. After being refused entry, he is given a souvenir and sent away. When he returns to his kingdom, he finds that no matter how much gold and silver he measures on a scale opposite his souvenir, the souvenir outweighs it. Curious as to the nature of the object, he consults with the Rabbis. They tell him that his souvenir is none other than a human eye, and if he will only sprinkle some dust over the eye, the gold and silver will quickly tip the scale.

The souvenir was in fact a powerful message to Alexander the Great. The reason he was not permitted access to the garden was in order that he not eat from the Tree of Life and gain immortality. The human condition is such that it allows man no satisfaction in this life. All the gold and silver in the world is not enough to satiate the human eye. Only in the grave does the eye find an end to its endless craving. The Rabbis admit to man's insatiable appetite for possessions, "one who has 100 desires to have 200!"[13] Only in death can man find solace.

With the Tree of Life completely off limits, our only alternative is to exist within the limits of the Tree of Knowledge. The difficulty in doing so is that the road we are left with is not an easy one. We are thrust upon the wine press. But there is hope, too, in the wine press. The *gittis* is used as a metaphor for man's ability to evolve. Man begins his journey through life as a seed, and soon progresses into a substantial offspring, capable of modest but earnest achievements. Similar to the grape on the vine, he will either be picked or simply continue to ripen until eventually rotting away. It is only through the great wine press of life that man can transcend his prosaic destiny and become, "... only slightly lower than the angels".[14] The trials and tribulations that befall man on this earth work as a human press to extract and refine the latent abilities lurking within his degenerate exterior. Man's main objective is not to be eaten straight off the vine, but to be pressed to the limit and left to ferment until he has reached his full potential and is ripe to serve as an ever-so-sweet beverage before the King of Kings.

While many oils and libations are extracted via pressing, only wine is given a special, elevated blessing. Upon the grape itself, we proclaim the same blessing given to all fruits: 'Blessed is the creator of fruits of the tree'. The grape's juice, however, is blessed with a unique formula extolling its origin as a 'fruit of the vine'. Perhaps the reference to 'vine' instead of 'tree' hints to one major characteristic of wine. Wine has its origins not as a fruit of a mighty tree, but in the crawling vine. While a tree can soar high into the sky, a vine cannot even bear its own weight. It must be supported by others. It is from this lowly beginning that the holiest libation derives.

Therefore the wine, which began as our nemesis, has become our partner. We extol the virtue of the fruit of the vine at every opportunity and expression of holiness. Although wine may have brought mortality to the world, it also represents an existence beyond time. While the nature of mortality is the weakening and eventual death of an object through time, wine was given the quality of improving over time. The longer wine ages, the better it becomes. When we raise our cup and sanctify the Sabbath or a wedding, or any of the myriad events where wine is blessed, we are affirming our belief that mortality can be beaten. As we hold the cup of wine in the palm of our hands we are reminded that eternity is not beyond our grasp. Unfortunately, the message can become convoluted, and throughout history attempts at short-cutting the refining and aging process of the wine message have been met with disaster.

Ten generations after Adam's blunder, Noah makes an attempt to set things straight. At that time, God decided that the earth had taken self-objectification to such extreme levels, there was no hope of getting mankind back on track. The commentators tell us that the overriding sins of the generation were those of illicit sexual relations and robbery. The people's bodies were nothing more than objects of their desires, and their desires extended to the objects of others. So with a heavy heart God decided to wipe out His subjects and all their objects, "from man to every beast".[15] Rashi comments on this verse: since all was created as man's object, what good were they without man as subject?

Yet, one man finds *chein/favor* in God's eyes. His name is the word *chein* ('chet', 'nun') spelled backwards. Noah means 'rest'. Speaking of Noah ('nun', 'chet') the verse reads, "[Noah] will bring us *rest* from our work and from the toil of our hands, from the ground which God had cursed".[16] In other words, it was time for the punishment given to Adam to be revoked. Life would once again become hospitable. Even the letters *chet-nun* themselves make this point. *Chet* represents the number eight, and nun represents the number fifty. Eight is the first number after the number seven, and fifty is the first number after forty-nine, which is seven times seven. Thus, both eight and fifty are numbers that represent the idea of ascending beyond the natural world, which was created in seven days. As Noah becomes the second 'first human', he correctly sees the opportunity to reform reality and eradicate the ill effects of the first sin.

When God created Adam, He initially gave him no mate. He brought all the animals before him for naming; a naming that would ultimately leave Adam exasperated and lonely. After examining the nature of every creature, Adam recognized their unique characteristics as objects in his reality. He found no creature with which he could stand as an equal and share his status as the lone subject among a universe of objects. There was a world full of helpful objects; what Adam craved was a fellow subject: a partner. Adam had now uncovered the crucial 'subject/object' paradigm and was made painfully aware of his lonely status as a subject. Once that understanding was reached, Adam was ready to meet his mate: his '*ezer kenegdo*' (helper of equal footing).

It is no coincidence that Noah was indoctrinated using the same method as Adam. He was first forced to learn to relate to the world as objects. He had to collect and care for every manner of beast, fowl and vermin. It was this grounding of his subjectness that made him think he could recapture the lost opportunities offered in the Garden and raise a new breed of man wherein the subject of each individual person is preserved.

That is why we are told that after the flood, Noah "planted a vineyard".[17] Why a vineyard? In his quest to recreate the conditions of primordial man, he found it necessary to replant the Tree of Knowledge. In his possession, Noah had a sampling of the Tree of Knowledge, which had been passed down to him through the ages.

Instead of accepting the harsh reality that man must embrace his self-conscious, egocentric nature, and work his way to salvation, Noah tried to rewind the actions of his predecessor and find a shortcut back to the Garden. While pre-sin man was pure subject, as evidenced by his unabashed nakedness, until he ate from the tree, Noah attempted to prove his ability to avoid objectification, by uncovering his nakedness after drinking from his vine. He wrongly assumed he could cancel the objectification of man's entity by entering altered states of consciousness. Noah's attempt to solidify his role as subject only strengthened his position as an object. His nakedness brought him to the depths of moral depravity. According to many sources, Noah, in his drunken stupor, is made the object of his son's desire. Cham, Noah's youngest son, sodomizes his father.

While man must accept his fallen state and work within the confines of his corporeal condition, the Torah does grant one person a slight respite from the ever-present wine press, and provide a shortcut to a holier state. However, it does not involve an indulgence in wine, but an abstinence from it.

The *Nazir* is granted permission back into the Garden. So long as he shuns the 'forbidden fruit', (no wine is drunk), avoids self-objectification (by not cutting his hair), and distances himself from mortality (by refusing contact with any corpse), he can stroll the rarefied paths of the Garden of Eden.

His stay in the Garden, however, is only temporary. The lifestyle of the *Nazir* is regarded more like a concession by *Halakhah* than a preferred approach — evidenced by the requirement that a *Nazir* bring a sin offering at the completion of his term. Furthermore, life-long *Nezirut* was observed only in very rare instances. It seems there is no true escape from life's demanding and exacting wine press.

There is one circumstance where *Nazirut* is not an option but a requirement. Upon seeing the humiliating and degrading ordeal imposed upon a woman, whose husband suspects her of marital infidelity, a person must accept a vow of *Nazirut*. The manner in which her guilt or innocence is proven involves striping the woman of her worth as a subject and revealing her place as an object. Witnessing such demoralizing treatment of another human being requires the therapeutic, albeit extreme, conditions of the vow of *Nazirut*.

While a *Nazir* can find his way back to the Garden, his

וַיְהִי בִּימֵי
אֲחַשְׁוֵרוֹשׁ

stay there is short lived. For a lasting reversal of the effects of the forbidden fruit we can not look for shortcuts back to Eden, instead, we must travel to a place called Shushan, the capital city of the Persian Empire, around 500 BCE. There, the Jewish people found themselves slated for annihilation. The cause of the fateful decree? An over-indulgence in, none other than: wine.

In Shushan, as in Eden, there are three main characters: a man, a woman, and a villain. But the similarities do not end there...

To recap: in the Garden we find an evil entity, the snake, enticing a woman, Eve, to destroy mankind, Adam. (The Rabbis say that the snake was romantically interested in Eve, and his motivation in getting her to take from the tree was to ultimately have Adam eat from the tree and die). As a result of Adam and Eve's having succumbed to the snake's ploy, they acquired a debilitating knowledge and forsook the Tree of Life. They were forced to accept a life of suffering as mere mortals.

In Shushan, as detailed in *Megillat Esther*, and commemorated with the holiday of Purim, we find the man, Mordechai, trying to convince the woman, Esther, to destroy the evil Haman. (As with Noah, Esther is also adorned with the word *chein* (favor) as it says, "Esther would find *favor* in the eyes of all who saw her").[18]

Threads woven throughout the Purim story can be pulled straight from the Garden of Eden. For example, the *Megillah* opens with the King requesting his queen, Vashti, to attend his party wearing nothing but her crown. She is stricken by embarrassment, and refuses. The Rabbis make the point that under normal circumstances the queen would have been happy to comply. Her embarrassment was a new-found anomaly. The requirement that she remove her clothing, as well as her surprising embarrassment at the thought, hearkens back to the nakedness and embarrassment experienced by the first couple, Adam and Eve.

With that one thread loosened, the fabric gives way, revealing a number of striking parallels between Shushan and Eden. The Rabbis tell us that references to 'the King' in the *Megillah* can be understood as referring to the King of Kings. When the King finds out that the wicked Haman is trying to destroy Queen Esther, the *Megillah* records a 'break in the action' of sorts and almost spells out a time travel back to the garden. "And the King rose in his anger from the wine feast and went into the palace garden".[19] In the garden, the Rabbis tell us that he saw the groundskeeper uprooting all the trees. Upon further inquiry, he is told that Haman had requested the uprooting; a not-so-subtle reminder that way back when, in the first garden, it was a similar villain who instigated the breach of the Tree of Knowledge, uprooted civilization and brought death and expulsion to the world. Instead of cooling his temper, the stroll in the garden brings back bad memories. So when the King returns from the garden, and finds Haman upon Esther's bed he accuses Haman in a redundant manner, "additionally, you attempt to subdue my queen?" The memory of the original seduction by the snake upon the woman has been rekindled by the garden stroll.

So what is the secret about Purim that made it a success when all other attempts at *tikun* (rectification) of Eden failed? There is one pivotal point in the Purim narrative where we can identify many of the themes we have been speaking of. Mordechai refuses to allow the tides of circumstance to wash his people out to sea. The tables must be turned on evil and Mordechai must convince Esther to see herself as more than an object, subject to the whims of the world at large. She is an integral part of a universality — a people. As Mordechai says, "Do not imagine in your soul that you will be able to escape in the King's palace any more than the rest of the Jews".[20] He then goes on to assure her that salvation will come with or without her. It's not about her alone, it's about the Jewish people. Yet, in the same message, he assures her that her individual worth is crucial: "Who knows, if for this time in particular, you have attained royalty?" As subjects, every individual has a role, a part, and the possibility of making an impact on the universal.

Esther agrees to risk her life and present herself to the King unannounced; an act, that more often than not, would result in her execution. It would seem that her only hope would be to spare no makeup, don the finest gown, and be doused by the most savory fragrances. As she enters the King's chamber she must become the *object* of his desires. He must be enamored with her beauty and seduced by her charm. The odds may still be against her, for the King has already shown a disdain for the non-subservient with his execution of Vashti, but Esther knows her beauty got her into the palace, and it is her best shot at getting her plea heard. Or is it?

In a startling move, Esther decides to present herself, "counter to the law".[21] Once Mordechai shifted her focus off of her own manifestation as an object, he gave her the freedom to function, rather than fixate. Esther is now ready to accept her unique individuality and use it for the universal good. Instead of presenting King Ahasuerus with a stunning vision of herself, which should evoke the most favorable effect, she decides to fast for three days and enter the King's chamber dressed in royal garb but looking pale and worn. Esther tells Mordechai, "... I also will fast ... and as such [in that tired and hungry state] I will come to the King, counter to the law". The simple meaning of, 'counter to the law' could refer to the law of being invited for an audience with the King. However, as it comes on the heels of her decision to fast, we may understand Esther as saying that contrary to the laws of cause and effect, I am recognizing the limitations of such an existence, and will appeal to a higher order by negating my self-objectification.

Unlike the fate of the snake in Eden, Haman's plan in Shushan is thwarted. As a result of Esther's success, the Rabbis say the Jewish people actually acquired the Torah anew on Purim. As the Torah is called a 'Tree of Life', it is safe to say that on Purim we discovered a way to liberate ourselves from the destructive knowledge of good and evil, and found ourselves in a state of *Ad d'lo yodah/until we no longer 'know'*! For on Purim we are told to drink wine until we no longer can *know* the difference between the *good* Mordechai and the *evil* Haman. This is a clear reference to a reversal back to a state before we were burdened with the knowledge of *good* and *evil*. On the holiday of Purim we use wine as it was intended, and hope to reach the lofty level of *not* 'knowing'.

The balance being sought between the self and the universal is so precarious a position, perhaps a somewhat lengthy quote directly from Rabbi Joseph B. Soloveitchik is required. In his book entitled 'Halachik Man', Rav Soloveitchik expounds, "Man, initially, must cause himself to pass into actuality; he must completely realize the form of the species 'man'. However, once he has actualized this universal form, then, instead of having his own specific image obliterated, he acquires a particular form, an individual mode of existence, a unique personality and an active, creative spirit ... This outlook is truly striking in its paradoxical nature ... man does not remain fastened to the realm of the particular, but betakes himself to the realm of the universal, to the idea of the whole".[22]

This is not a denial of the self, but a denial of self-centeredness, or as we have been referring to it, a denial of self-objectification. The *Mishnah* in Sanhedrin says, *Kol echad V'echad chayav Lomar: 'Beshvili Nivrah ha'olam'/Every person is obligated to say, 'It is for me that the world was created'*. This is hardly an attempt at denying the self. What we must understand instead is that the *Mishna* wants man to realize he is not merely an object among a sea of objects, floating along at the mercy of the prevailing currents. Each and every one of us is capable of being the subject of our existence and denying our role as objects, thereby liberating our mundane lives to a level of serving the eternal, universal human race, rather than the wants and desires of a temporal individual. Schopenhauer describes it as such: "we no longer consider the where, the when, the whither of things, but simply and solely the what ... [We] let our whole consciousness be filled by the calm contemplation of the natural object actually present, whether it be a landscape, a tree, a rock, a crag, a building, or anything else ... and continue to exist only as pure subject".[23]

Man is left with the arduous task of embracing his individuality as a subject in a world of objects, while divesting it of any egoistic motivations, and still withstanding the tendency to be objectified by another's subjective gaze. The balancing act must be performed without a net, and for the most part completely blindfolded.

While philosophers can often leave their theories in the ether, never having to implement them, the striving individual must find a way to integrate the theories and presumptions into everyday life. Not all of us have the benefit of coming face to face with every creature on the planet, like Adam and Noah, in an effort to help us objectify the empirical world. And even fewer of us ever claim to hear the voice of God direct our actions. So how does one structure his life to maximize the potential creative power inherent in the subject/object dynamic?

Were it not for Rabbi Joseph B. Soloveitchik, this entire essay would most likely be an exercise in futility. Only he could find concrete expressions for the elusive ideas expressed as part of our exploration of the human condition. In Halakhic Man, Rav Soloveitchik puts Plato's, Kant's and Schopenhauer's notes to the beautiful music of the Torah. He eloquently shows the connection between Jewish Law's obsession with quantifying reality and Schopenhauer's theory of 'aesthetics'. Yet at the same time he is able to turn his back on core elements of philosophical theories, such as Schopenhauer's insistence on aesthetic's eradication of the 'will' in order to achieve some semblance of bliss. Rav Soloveitchik holds on to the primordial 'will', (not to be confused with the 'Will' sporting a capital 'W'). "for in the final analysis it is the will which is the source of freedom".[24]

With a few quotes from Rav Soloveitchik's, 'Halachik Man' we will attempt to wrap all these concepts into a formula capable of spanning the tightrope-walker's fearless tether. The goal, as stated by Rav Sloloveitchik, is the same as we have been referring to all along; "The creature must become the creator, the object who is acted upon a subject who acts".[25]

Rav Soloveitchik's secret weapon is the Law. "If a man wishes to attain the rank of holiness, he must become a creator of worlds ... Creation is the lowering of transcendence into the midst of our turbid, coarse, material world; and this lowering can take place only through the implementation of the ideal *Halakhah* in the core of reality". And how do you implement Halakhah in the core of reality?

"When the real world will conform to the ideal world and the most exalted and glorious of creations, the ideal *Halakhah*, will be actualized in its midst.[26] Man resembles somewhat the mathematician who masters infinity only for the sake of creating finitude, delimited by numbers and mathematical measures, and cognizing it. The *Halakhah* ... also uses the method of quantification; it quantifies quality and religious subjectivity in the form of concrete, objective phenomena that are standardized and measurable. What constitutes eating and what are its measurements, what constitutes drinking and what are its standards, what constitutes a fruit and what are its stages of development and distinguishing characteristics... and many more".[27]

While the winepress represents the forces of reality that come crashing down upon mankind, its produce, the wine, stands as a symbol for our ultimate salvation. Locked within the grape, the juice has a limited ability to reach sanctity. Once liberated from the confinement of the fruit, its status changes drastically. Its blessing is elevated, and it becomes an integral part of almost every spiritual event, from sanctifying the holy day to being offered in the holy Temple.

It is true that the wine press exerts much pressure and inflicts copious amounts of suffering, however, the alternative of simply living out our days and rotting on the vine, never having the opportunity to partner with the creator in completing His work of creation, and never unlocking our true potential as co-creators, might be an even greater injustice.

The Covenant

By comparing the mass deportations of the European Jews with Abraham's relocation from his birthplace, we uncovered a powerful example of a phenomenon the Ramban calls, *ma'ase avot siman l'banim/ the acts of our ancestors are a sign for future generations.* Abraham's, Isaac's and Jacob's lives can, and do, provide guidance and solace for future generations.

What our generation must realize, is that the Ramban's formula works just as well in reverse. There are descendants whose actions will standout as signs for the ancestors!

The Covenant Between the Parts was a ceremonial pact between God and Abraham. Abraham was well aware of life's dark side and feared that future generations would be unable to maintain the lifestyle of a chosen people. Abraham desperately sought reassurance that all the blessings God had promised him and his descendants would never be revoked.

A Covenant capable of spanning the gap between the Infinite and the finite requires a good measure of creativity, plenty of bloodshed, and a healthy dose of nerves. The Covenant is full of symbolism and open to interpretation. Let us look at a few of the major symbols, and how they might be understood.

God has Abraham split apart various animals and line their opposing parts in two parallel rows. Not all the sacrificed animals were to be split, however. Abraham was instructed not to split the *Tur* (turtledove) or the *Gozel* (young dove), but to leave them whole. Eventually birds of prey called *Ayit* (eagles) descended upon the carcasses, but not upon the *Tur* and the *Gozel*.

Rav Hirsch explains the significance of the bird offerings as symbolizing Israel's ability to survive despite the persecutions of the nations. "The bird is that creature which has neither strength nor power but which, nevertheless, by its ability to take wing, is able to escape man's sphere of power. Hence it symbolizes a timid, ephemeral but free form of existence for which snares are skillfully laid but which is able to avoid entrapment by means of its wings ... 'But the birds he did not divide'. This symbolized that *Hashem* allowed only the inner strength,

the spiritual entity to take wing, remain unbroken, and soar above misery".[1]

Following Rav Hirsch's beautiful interpretation of the sacrificed birds representing the Jewish soul, we can perhaps attribute the other sacrificed animals as representations of the Jewish body. To me the symbolism is eerily reminiscent of the way the Nazi's inspected the newly arrived inmates, and sent some to the right and most to the left. Some would live to see another day and most would be sent to the gas chamber. The Jewish people themselves were physically ripped apart, split in half!

This would explain why Abraham must intercede and protect the other offerings from the swooping down upon the carcasses by the *Ayit* (a bird of prey), but not the *Tur* or the *Gozel*. The Germans succeeded in destroying the Jewish body, but the soul was untouchable. And why the *Ayit*? The German national bird is the *Ayit*. (Birds of prey are the national animal of over a dozen modern day countries, including the United States, so while it is not astonishing that Germany be represented by the *Ayit*, it is appropriate).

Through all this, the atmosphere continued to darken. The consolation Abraham sought seemed to be slipping away. His initial fears that his descendants would lose their faith and forfeit their chosen status seemed more and more likely.

God reveals to Abraham that the road to peace and tranquility will be a crooked road of detours. So many detours, that a great dread comes upon Abraham and he is overtaken by a deep sleep, and the setting of the sun leaves a great darkness.

It seems as if the reassurance Abraham was looking for was nowhere in sight. Abraham became intensely fearful that under such adverse circumstances no people could remain faithful.

Then somehow, amidst all this darkness, we are told that the dark turns to pitch. Just when Abraham thought he had reached the abyss, he is blinded by the abysmal. As the verse relates, "The Sun [now] set, and it was *very* dark".[2] Abraham's initial dread and failure to remain hopeful was now reflected in a complete visual breakdown. In some metaphysical way, Abraham is made to feel the full depth of the abandonment awaiting his descendants.

With just one trick left up its sleeve, the Covenant seems incapable of assuaging Abraham's fears and insecurities. The one trick left: a smoky furnace and a lit torch appear out of nowhere in between the parts. Abraham is shown, "... a smoky furnace and a torch of fire".

The climax of the covenant has been reached, ratification is complete. Somehow, this ends the encounter, lifts the veil of darkness and resolves the issue. But does it? How can it? The build-up leading to God's revelation of the furnace and the torch is far more impressive than the solace offered by a couple of incendiary devices. Doesn't Abraham deserve more? Don't we expect to find the darkness not only brightened, but completely enlightened?

So earth-shattering is this vision, that the *Zohar*[3] tells us it was alluded to in the first word of the Torah.

We find, in the name of Rabbi Abba, that the first covenant between God and His Creation was with *aish/fire*, as it says in regard to the *Covenant Between the Parts*', "Behold a smoking furnace and a burning torch that passed between those pieces".[4] And this is indicated clearly in the first word of the Torah, '*Beraishit*', where the third and fourth letters, *alef* and *shin*, spell '*aish*', which is surrounded by the first and second letters, *beis* and *reysh*, and the fifth and sixth letters, *yud* and *taf*, spelling '*Brit*' (covenant).

There are examples found throughout the Torah where a dialogue between God and man seems to end abruptly and without a clear resolution. In the story of Jonah, for example, we are supposed to be satisfied with the lesson of a dead vine. Jonah is close to suicide and somehow the dead vine is supposed to bring him back from the brink. Does it work? One can only assume that the absence of a response indicates the matter has been laid to rest. Here too, just when the darkness has become completely opaque, the emergence of a 'smoking furnace and a lit torch' symbolizes complete resolution of the matter. And just like the vine in Jonah's case, the image is so clear and definitive that there is no need to record a response from Abraham.

So what does this image symbolize? How does it inform Abraham that his fears concerning the spiritual fortitude of his descendants are unfounded? And why immortalize this solution in the first word of the Torah?

The traditional view is that the *Shechina/divine presence*, is represented by the oven and flame. It passes through the pieces and conveys a reassurance that it will always honor its promise to give the land to the Jewish people. Abraham was under the impression that the promise was merit-based, and God shows him that it is a gift, deserved or not, and will never be rescinded.

Perhaps the choice of a furnace and a torch, however, have a specific connotation all their own. Of all the objects that could represent the *Shechina*, these two beg for interpretation.

I suggest the following: The final unbearable darkness represents the greatest cataclysm to befall man. Abraham was exposed to all the exiles and oppressions, but in the end the Holocaust may have been too much to bear.[5] Surely, thought Abraham, his descendants would lose their faith under such conditions.

As for the smoking furnace and lit torch? Might a smoking furnace be the perfect symbol for a gas chamber? The lit torch a crematorium? If so, the Covenant between the parts is none other than a preview into this absolute lowest point in Jewish history. Clearly represented are the three main components of Hitler's 'final solution:' the selection process, the gassing and the burning.

As compelling a comparison as this all is, how does it finally bring solace to our Patriarch? How is it possible to find a silver lining in such a dark, dark place?

Abraham is gripped with fear and dread when he is shown a sampling of the horrors that lie ahead. Perhaps he sees millions of his great-granddaughters being forced into smoking furnaces and gassed to death with their offspring clenched tightly in their arms. In such a vision there cannot possibly be any consolation.

Not in the vision, but perhaps in the sound. It is not what Abraham saw that offered consolation — it was what he heard. He heard, not the cries of his people, but their voices. He heard their voices rise from the smoking furnace in a chorus that would make the famous phrase '*Na'aseh VeNeshma*' pale by comparison. His children entered the gas chambers with the song *I Believe* emanating from their vocal cords, and spent their absolute final breath proclaiming God's unity together with their suffocating children, held tightly in their trembling arms.

The heroic acts of faith exhibited by the generation of the Shoah are a clear sign for the patriarch Abraham that it was not for naught that God chose the Jewish people to be his own. This stiff-necked nation will never forsake their God, and therefore the covenant would never be voided, rescinded, or otherwise violated.

Abraham is indeed consoled. The Covenant provides Abraham the assurance he needed, but why immortalize it in the first word of the Torah? Why form the word for, 'In the beginning' out of two words alluding to the Covenant?

To better understand the connection, we must ask yet another question. This question is actually found in the first Rashi in the Torah, and is one of the most fundamental queries in Biblical scholarship. Rav Yitzchak asks, why does the Torah begin at the beginning? The Torah is not a story-book or a history-book, but a book of law. As such, it would make more sense to begin the Torah with the first commandment placed upon the Congregation of Israel: blessing the new moon. According to Rav Yitzchak, the Torah must begin with creation in order to silence any claim by the nations that Israel's conquest of the Land of Canaan is an act of thievery. By establishing God as the Creator, He then has the right to give and take land as He sees fit. Israel's inheritance of the land is therefore legitimate.

Rav Yerucham sees much more insight in Rav Yizchak's question and answer than merely a response to hostile nations. After all, what kind of an answer is it? Try telling any of Israel's enemies that the Jewish people have a God-given right to the land, and see if it makes any difference at all. Instead, Rav Yerucham interprets Rav Yitzchak's message in broader terms. From the very first word of the Torah we are to understand that life is not *hefker/meaningless* or *directionless*. There is a purpose to it all. History is flowing in a direction towards a final goal. Heaven and earth and everything in them were created so that the Land of Canaan could be inherited by the Jewish people. It's not just that the Creator has a right to give the land to anyone He pleases, and it happens to please Him to give it to the people of Israel. Rather, we are to understand that from the *beginning* it was God's plan to have His people inhabit the Holy Land.

That is what Rav Yitzchak means when he makes the connection between creation at the beginning of the Torah and settling the land at the end of the Torah. The entire Torah is one journey towards a single goal.

Now we can understand why the first word in the Torah alludes to the Covenant. The Covenant narrative connects the stewardship of the Land of Israel with the fulfillment of the Covenant, "On that day *Hashem* made a covenant with Abram, saying, 'To your descendants have I given this land'". The Covenant, like creation, was all about the land.

So if indeed the vision Abraham was shown at the covenant was that of the Holocaust, one might expect a fulfillment of that covenant to be not far off. And, in an unprecedented move, just a few short years after the end of the Holocaust, the United Nations, made up of the very nations Rav Yitzchak was referring to, granted the Jewish people an independent rule of the Land of Israel!

Baggage

The great pre-creation void gives way to heaven and earth in order to allow the children of Israel to inherit the land of Israel. Possessing the land serves God's ultimate agenda of making His presence known throughout the world. But what purpose is served by man's labor for material possessions? Besides land, one can possess objects. The material world around us can be acquired and possessed. But to what end are such pursuits? Does our amassing *stuff* amount to anything worthwhile?

With little or no warning, the Nazis rounded up their captives and herded them onto the cattle cars. If a family had time, they threw what they could into a suitcase and held on to hope that this was relocation rather than extermination.

The image of one's belongings abandoned by the tracks conjures up a sense of empathy for its owners. These people hoped against hope that they would still have a need for their precious few earthly possessions. Instead, their possessions outlived them and now stand orphaned by the railway tracks.

In reality, don't we all leave behind our possessions? We don't all face the tragedy of a life cut short, but from the minute we are born our lives are a runaway train headed straight for the grave. Yet we toil, sweat and save — for what?

The Rabbis assure us that we will not leave this world with more than half our desires fulfilled. Therefore, the more we have, the more we are lacking. If we have 100, we only wish for another hundred. But if we have 500 we want a thousand, leaving us $400 further from our goal and psychologically $400 poorer than when we only had $100! The more possessions we have the less at ease we are. With an increase in possessions comes an equal share of aggravation. It would seem that amassing any sort of wealth is an exercise in futility.

Is Judaism then, an ascetic faith?

Enter, Honi HaMagil, the circle drawer, so called because he once drew a circle in the ground and vowed not to leave the confines of his self-imposed circumference until the heavens give forth an abundance of rain. Of the many tales expounded upon in the Talmud, few characters are as interesting as Honi HaMagil. He challenges God, is threatened with excommunication by the Rabbis, sleeps for 50 years longer than Rip Van Winkle, and eventually begs God to kill him.

We begin when Honi HaMagil meets a man who is planting carob trees.[1] Curious, Honi asks him, "How long will it take for the tree to bear fruit?"

"70 years", is the reply.

"Do you really expect to live that long?" asks Honi.

"When I looked around, I saw carob trees planted by the last generation for my enjoyment. Therefore, I will plant carob trees for the next generation", was the man's answer.

This story is almost universally understood as a perfect example of social consciousness. Existence did not begin with our birth, nor does it end with our death. We are a link in a chain, and we have a social responsibility to preserve that chain. Our possessions indeed survive us and benefit subsequent generations. Instead of an unhappy ending, we have an everlasting succession. Our possessions are not abandoned, they are inherited.

Where, then, does this chain lead? If every generation is another link, what exactly are we connected to? Is there a final generation so worthy that I should live out my years so that they will be able to live theirs? If my father existed for me, and I exist for my children — if mine was the last generation, would my existence matter?

In *Kohellet*, King Solomon asks, "What profit does man have for all his labor which he toils beneath the sun?"[2]

Let us answer him with our link-in-a-chain concept: possessions are passed down.

To that King Solomon says, "A generation goes and a generation comes, but the earth endures forever.[3] Thus I hated all my achievements laboring under the sun, for I must leave it to the man who succeeds me".[4]

Honi parts company with the carob tree planter without making a comment. We are left in the dark as to how he feels about the man's pursuits. We need to look at the story in context with the incidents that precede it as well as those that follow it if we hope to gain some kind of understanding.

Leading up to Honi's rendezvous with the Talmudic version of Johnny Appleseed, we are told that Honi was troubled his whole life by a phrase in Psalms, "When the Lord will return the captivity of Zion, we will be like dreamers".[5] The reference here is to the Babylonian exile which lasted 70 years. Honi could not accept the premise of this verse. As he understood it, it was saying that it was possible for a man to dream for seventy years. As we see in another Psalm, the reference to 70 years actually can represent the totality of one's life, "... the days of a man are seventy years".[6] Therefore, on a deeper level he was understanding the verse to mean that all a man's endeavors throughout his lifetime could be as meaningless as a dream.[7] Are our earthly pursuits utterly futile? Do the possessions we leave behind as our legacy to the next generation simply mock us?

It is at this point that Honi meets up with Johnny 'Carobseed'. But things get even stranger when the two part ways. At that point, Honi falls into a deep sleep. A sleep lasting... you guessed it... 70 years! When he wakes, he is surrounded by mature carob trees and sees the grandson of Johnny 'Carobseed', picking the fruit from the trees. He also finds his donkey has produced much offspring. But to Honi's dismay, no one in his hometown or the house of study recognizes him. Honi is mortified. In fact, he is moved to seek relief from this world, and he dies.

A bizarre turn of events, but what does it all mean, and how does this relate to our question of the value of material possessions and the material world?

Honi's adventure is an existential one. He grapples with the possibility that a man's life could be no more than a series of illusions. As one wakes from a dream and has no remnants left over from his nocturnal endeavors, so too a man could live out his years and in the end have nothing to show for it. When a starving man sleeps, and dreams he is eating, does he wake in a satiated state? If life is but a dream, what's the point?

The Talmud tells us that Honi's 'circle' actually mimics the prophet Habakuk's 'circle'. Habakuk is troubled by the success of the wicked and draws a circle from which he vows not to leave until God explains His ways. The connection between Honi and Habakuk runs even deeper than their shared admiration for the circle. Legend has it that Habbakuk is the son of the Shunnamite woman who showed kindness to Elisha, and in return for her efforts, Elisha blesses her with a son. This son is stricken at a young age and actually dies. Elisha has to resurrect the boy. This child grows to be Habbakuk.[8] The link between the Shunnamite woman, Habbakuk and Honi HaMagil is that they all demand that life live up to their expectations. What they put into life they should receive back from life. The Shunnamite woman demands Elisha revive the boy with the phrase, "Did I ask for a son? Did I not say, 'Do not mislead me?'"[9] In Habbakuk's prophecy we find a similar sentiment, "How long will I cry out, and you not hear me?"[10] And Honi likewise, demands that reality synchronize with his prayers, "It is not for this that I had prayed!"[11] They all feel misled, and what's more, they all seem to feel an entitlement to have life play out according to their understanding. 2 + 2 = 4. They put the 'real' in 'reality'. That's why Honi is so disturbed by the notion that existence could be dreamlike in nature.

Habbakuk's and Honi's use of the circle is appropriate. The circle is the most common geometric shape in the material world. It is the only shape whose every point is equidistant from the center point. It can also be viewed as a line whose end meets up with its beginning. A representation of cause and effect, and harmony. This equanimity is exactly what the Shunnamite woman,

Habbakuk, and Honi, live for.

In the Hebrew alphabet, the letter represented by a circle is the *Samech*. The *Samech* is understood in mystical terms as the letter of support. Reality is something you can count on, rely on, and should be able to understand. In Honi's world there is a logical succession of events. 'A' precedes 'B', 'B' precedes 'C' and so on.

Honi was comforted by an existence that made rational sense. In his famous story as a 'rainmaker' he challenged heaven to bring rain. In his mind, it was logical that if the people were thirsty, the rains should fall. With absolute confidence, Honi demanded the heavens open up and pour down on the parched land.

Honi refuses to accept a life devoid of tangible meaning. But if we analyze the events in Honi's adventure, we find a pattern of the absurd. The Carob tree is the most barren of all fruit-bearing trees. It stands as the symbol of meager rations.[12] Yet it is this tree the man exerts his energy to propagate. Should a man work his whole life and not live to enjoy the fruits of his labor? This sort of injustice does not make sense to the 'rainmaker'. Honi's donkey further illustrates life's futile nature by giving birth to mules. A mule can not reproduce; it is a sterile creature. Upon waking, Honi sees that his donkey has expended itself, not in a sustainable effort to propagate the species, but towards a short-lived, limited expression. Again, an exercise in futility. Finally Honi finds that he is completely unrecognizable to the current society. The miraculous 'rainmaker' has awoken to find he has nothing to show for his illustrious career. These examples illustrate an irrational approach to life. In our dreamlike existence 2 + 2 doesn't always equal 4. Sometimes 2 + 2 = 0. Our efforts amount to nothing; our achievements to less than nothing.

King David deals with Honi's concerns and somehow finds a point to it all. Psalm 17 conjures up various themes that are found in Habbakuk's prophecy, and in the end King David accepts the notion that life is like a dream. It is this dream state that moves King David to shun the accumulation of material possessions, "... let them have children in plenty and let them leave their abundance to their offspring".[13] Instead, King David concludes, "As for me, I shall behold thy face in thoughts of the right, and when one day I awaken, I shall be satisfied with thy formation". King David accepts life as irrational and incomprehensible — as absurd. But he will continue to exist inside the dream and accept the fantasy that is the human condition.

One cannot however ignore the fact that the Shunnamite woman, Habbakuk, and Honi, all end up getting their way. If their insistence on a sensible reality is unreasonable, why do they meet with such extraordinary success? It says that there are three keys God retains for himself. He alone controls birth, resurrection, and rainfall. It is precisely these activities that are manifest in our three personalities. Birth is a special blessing given to the Shunnamite woman, Habbakuk is resurrected, and Honi is a rainmaker.

I believe their success comes precisely from their ability to demand life work out. Each held such a total belief in a fair God, that they could not tolerate injustice. The only way the rest of us can 'carry-on' is by

numbing ourselves to the harsh reality of an incoherent existence. We must exist in some form of a coma to be able to serve a God that grants so much success to the forces of evil. Holocausts, pogroms and crusades should not be easily digested as norms in a divinely driven universe. We should be shaken to our knees, we should be opting for a way out of this madness. The Shunnamite woman's, Habbakuk's, and Honi's, refusal to accept these 'realities' proves they had a complete belief in a righteous, caring God. As we have said elsewhere, according to Albert Camus, the French Existentialist writer, "only through rebellion do we prove our belief in that which we rebel against".

For most, the God of righteousness is a concept not a reality. We tolerate injustice because we hardly believe in God. They, however, were brave enough to live with eyes wide open; while the bulk of us must shield our eyes from a reality we cannot comprehend.

One thing seems to hold true, both for Honi and the wide-awake amongst us, and for David and the dreamers amongst us, for material pursuits to have any value at all, they must provide a benefit to the laborer himself.

Expending the grains of sand in one man's hourglass simply to fill anothers, is truly an exercise in futility.

Is there any way that the amount of energy we expend on material pursuits could be of value?

Shimon bar Yochai, the author of the mystical work the *Zohar* can lead us out of our dilemma. For twelve years, he and his son hid from the Roman enemy in a cave. A miracle occurred and a carob tree suddenly appeared and a spring of water burst forth nearby. All day they would learn Torah together uninterrupted by any disturbances. After having spent twelve years in the cave, fully immersed in learning Torah, Eliyahu HaNovi appeared at the entrance of the cave and notified them that the Roman Emperor had died and therefore all prisoners were granted an automatic pardon to return home.

As they began their walk back into town, they noticed a farmer plowing and planting a field. "Why is he wasting his precious time preparing for his needs for this world when he ought to spend his valuable time making preparations for the world to come?" Rav Shimon bar Yochai wondered. He looked at the farmer with his penetrating holy eyes and the man immediately turned into a heap of bones. Thereupon a heavenly voice called out, "Do you want to destroy my world? Go back to the cave. The world is unable to exist with your great holiness". Shimon bar Yochai and his son returned for one more year in the cave totally immersed in Torah.[14]

The Talmud doesn't tell us what it was that Rav Shimon bar Yochai learned in that extra year that enabled him to endure the sight of material pursuits. Did he modify his stance, and understand the value of temporal efforts, or did he maintain his disdain, but learn to be tolerant of those engaged in such pursuits?

Perhaps it is not what he learned in those twelve months, but what he saw when he left the cave that altered his perception. At the end of the additional year the pair went out and sat down at the entrance to the cave, where they saw a trapper attempting to catch birds by spreading his net. When they heard a divine voice say, 'mercy, mercy' the bird escaped, and when they heard the voice say, 'death', the bird was trapped and stayed caught. Rav Shimon bar Yochai witnessed the intense relationship heaven has with the dealings of man. Material pursuits needn't be profane. They can also provide the purest examples of a clinging to the Divine. With the proper motivation, the work of our hands can be the expression of our hearts.

So vital are economic pursuits to divine service that we find a drastic example of heavenly excommunication brought about by the lack of material efforts. When the snake of the Garden of Eden is punished for his involvement in the first sin, he is smitten with a new diet. He is to sustain himself on nothing more than the dust of the earth. The snake has economic security everywhere he turns. Yet we must keep in mind that this situation is a curse, not a blessing. The snake has no opportunity to promote a relationship between himself and the Creator. The Kotsker Rav put it succinctly; God provided the snake with a livelihood and then told him to get out of His sight. Our dependence on support from God for a livelihood gives us practically unlimited access to the divine presence.

Similarly, the Jewish exile had to be in Egypt where all economic bounty depended not on rain, but on the Nile. The flooding of the water of the Nile provided Egypt with its sustenance, while it is rain that supports most of the rest of mankind. The eyes of the Egyptians therefore would always be turned to the ground. Everywhere else, rain comes from heaven, so men lift their eyes to heaven, send their praise to God, and God sends down rain to provide for them. In Egypt there was no spiritual relationship between man and God in the economic sphere. In order to construct a proper ethical society, the Jews had to learn this lesson. Perforce, their exile was to be in Egypt.[15]

Even the Jewish nation, when on the cusp of inheriting the land, (the objective of all creation as we have determined in the previous essay), were thwarted by concerns of an economic nature. According to Shmuel of Sochochow (Poland, early 20th century) the reason the spies, sent to scout out the land, returned with a negative report, was that they felt they were not up to the challenge of economic norms. They preferred the falling Manna and miraculous Well of Miriam for their sustenance.

It would seem that the pursuit itself of material possessions is of value to mankind. And that is why the Talmud says, "Regarding the righteous, their property is more precious to them than their own bodies".[16] Why? Answers the Talmud, "Because they do not stretch out their hands in acts of thievery".[17] They must instead forge that relationship with God and learn to relate to the Righteous God of the Shunnamite woman, of Habbakuk, and of Honi HaMagil.

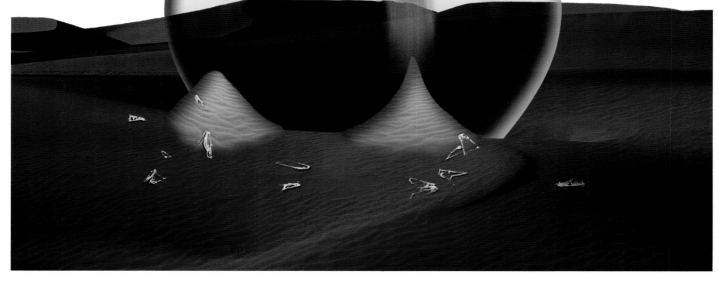

Culture Shock

One of the most surprising components of the Nazi regime is that Germany was a nation on the cusp of cultural aristocracy. They were not savages; they had produced symphonies, works of art, and scientific breakthroughs of the highest order. How, then, did they commit genocide?

Rabbinic tradition teaches that often the purest meaning of a word or concept can be gleaned by a close examination of the first appearance it makes in the Torah. Murder makes an early appearance in man's history. The very first man born of woman is none other than a murderer. Cain commits fratricide; effectively wiping out half of his generation. He wasted no time seizing the opportunity to rid the earth of what he considered was 'undesirable' (reminiscent of an 'Aryan Race' mentality).

A casual reading of the incident reveals a story about a jealous brother who, in a fit of rage, spills his brother's blood — a simple crime of passion. The Kli Yakar, a 16th century commentator, sees much more to the story. The details are fragmentary, but the Torah makes a point of telling us that the gruesome act took place: "At the end of days".[1] What is meant by the "end of days"? According to the Kli Yakar, the "end of days" in this context, refers to *what*, not *when!* The phrase refers not to when the scene took place, rather to why it took place. He says that Cain and Abel were actually engaged in an existential debate of the highest order.

The question the Kli Yakar places at the center of their dispute is no less than: what takes precedence in a man's life, this world or the next? Cain favored the here and now, while Abel preferred waiting for the next round.

In order to settle the dispute, they offered sacrifices to God and awaited His response. Cain offered produce from the earth, signifying his belief in the concrete, tangible present. Abel chose to bring a sacrifice from among his herd, which roams freely and is not tied down to any specific locale. Abel gives precedence to those things a person can 'take' with him. His view of this world could be likened to the opinion of the sages: this world is simply a corridor to the great banquet hall that is the next.

Cain could have argued that there is no mention of a 'next world' in the Torah, and our focus must remain on where we are, not where we are going. Cain may have been a strong believer in a next world, but his path to that next world ran through different terrain than that of his brother. The road to paradise is paved by the sweat and toil of mortal man. This world is where the action is and man is center stage.

Cain proved his point by bringing God a sacrifice comprised of the fruits of man's labor. He specifically chose inferior fruits, for he reasoned that even the weakest of man's efforts were more precious to God than an offering of better quality, but little human effort. Cain was the Nietzsche of his time, "God is dead, long live the *Überman*". It is not that he didn't believe in God; rather he believed that man must make it in this world on his own. Man must control his own destiny, with no cosmic forces to stand in his way. God created the world in six days and then He rested. Now we are to take over. God is not a crutch to be leaned on by feeble man. Cain is self-supporting and proud. He doesn't need to cop out and put his faith in God. Such luxury is not man's lot. We are to use all our own faculties to develop and succeed. Ethics?...man-made. Morals and laws?...man-made. As philosophers of the Enlightenment put it; man is "infinitely perfectible". The Germans called this concept: '*Aufklärung*'.

So when Cain's sacrifice is denied in favor of his brother's, in a clear preference for Abel's world view, Cain is left decimated. He is uprooted to the very core of his existence.

Obviously we are not dealing with cavemen embroiled in a popularity contest. Cain and Abel represent mankind at its intellectual peak. And yet, Cain, the great philosopher, had no qualms acting like a butcher. Similarly, along the banks of the Rhine walked the cultural elite, yet, at the end of the day the river ran red with innocent blood.

Sometimes the ends may justify the means, but can the means ever justify the ends?

Cain's *means* actually make a lot of sense. Much like Nietzsche's *Überman*, his man, is a 'man's man': capable, powerful and ultimately responsible. It is just these *means* which the patriarch Isaac saw and loved in his son Esau.

In the whole narrative of Cain and Abel, very little is made of Abel. He is merely Cain's foil. God's attention is riveted on Cain. In fact, after rejecting Cain's world view, God clearly still favors him over his brother.[2] When God informs Cain that he need not be despondent, and he can indeed succeed, our sages interpret God's words with an interesting twist. God isn't telling Cain to abandon his evil ways. Instead he is telling him to temper his ways. Cain, the *Überman*, can succeed and can even excel, if only he change his focus. Keep the fire in his soul, but stoke it with the will of God. As it says, "I have created man's passion, and I have created the Torah as its spice".[3] Notice, the Torah is not the main dish, but its status is that of a spice with which to add flavor to the main dish. Cain should not be depressed. He is very close to the truth. Unfortunately, in existential terms, close is not near. The slightest deviation will evolve into a vast expanse. Before Cain will be able to get one foot out the door, the evil will pounce on him, "Sin crouches at the door".[4] When you rely on your own conventions as a guiding force in life, the apex of your development will be brutal, savage bloodshed. When you insist on home rule over heaven rule, sin crouches at your door, waiting to pounce.

We see this lesson played out in Cain's denial of any wrongdoing. When confronted with the crime, the Kli Yakar understands Cain's words of, "am I my brother's keeper?" as a claim by Cain that he was never told not to murder. Here Cain is trying to have it both ways. His philosophy dictates that man alone must determine what is right and wrong, yet in his defense he claims he had violated no divine prohibition. No one ever told him not to kill his brother. Or in other words, the Nazi soldiers were just 'following orders', they are blameless.

At this point God brings a bizarre reference to the ground's role in the murder. "The voice of your brother's blood cries out to me from the ground!"[5] How does this counter Cain's claim of blamelessness?

God is in essence using Cain's own philosophy against himself by proving such an act to be perverse even by human standards. No divine prohibition need be laid down to teach man not to murder. It is self evident. The blood cries out from nature itself. If your philosophy, which claims that man can deduce his own standard of ethics were right, then such a crime could never have happened. Obviously, Man without God is capable of fratricide and society without God — genocide.

Cain finally understands that man left to his own desires will ultimately lead to a total breakdown of morals. He admits that if indeed God abandons him now, his fate and the fate of all humanity is sealed, "and *all* who find me will kill me".[6] Why does Cain suppose that *all*

future people will kill him? Will they be moved by a sense of justice to avenge Abel's blood? God has already meted out a punishment! If anything, the fact that Cain didn't get away with it, should pacify future vigilantes. And who are these future men? They are none other than his own children. Is a man truly afraid of his own descendants?

Instead, Cain, with these words, is admitting to God that he was wrong. His *Weltanschauung* was corrupt. And now, that God has distanced Himself from Cain, and presumably all mankind, Cain's original philosophy is sure to take hold. His concern is not for his own well being, but for all mankind. Cain is saying that if indeed his original mode of thinking is adopted by man, there is no hope for *any* man. 'All' who find him, will kill him, because 'all' men left to their own devices will turn into murderers.

Still, it is not 'all' men with which we began our discussion, but specifically '*creative*' men. All men and women may be created equal, but some go beyond mere creature and are rightfully called creators. They infuse their lives with a spirit, a beauty, an expression of the Divine. It is this creative spirit which Rav Soloveitchik portrays as the divine spirit with which God imbued all humankind. Those who tap into their creative spirit and emulate their Creator draw near to God and by all rights should be beyond destructive behavior, let alone barbarism and genocide.

Or are they? If we turn the Cain and Abel story upside down and begin where it ends, we find a clear link between Cain the creator and Cain the murderer. In fact, it is specifically Cain's creative spirit which is blamed for his bloodthirsty ways. In response to Cain's murder of his brother, God finds it appropriate to strip Cain of nothing less than his creative spirit, "When you work the ground, it shall no longer yield its strength to you".[7] What's more, Cain finds this punishment more than he can bear, "My iniquity is greater than can be borne!"[8]

What are we to make of this direct link between the ability to create and the temptation to destroy?

If we accept Rav Soloveitchik's interpretation of man being created in the image of God, then we can begin to understand the double-edged sword that lies deep within the creative genius. The ability to act like God should inspire man towards Godly behavior. It should enable him to resist his animal instincts, and as King David puts it, "You have made him (man) slightly less than the angels".[9]

However, there is a dark side to all the splendor. In *Imitatio dei* one runs the risk of apotheosis, or self-deification. If man creates, not for God, but to be God, he is capable of horrors beyond imagination. Simply put, creativity for the sake of heaven elevates us above the beast, creativity for its own sake makes us the beast!

Apathy

When God inquires as to the whereabouts of Abel, Cain answers with a question: "am I my brother's keeper?" With these words Cain is not denying knowing where Abel is, rather, he hopes to deflect any responsibility for his brother's life and any guilt for his murder.

Almost cynically, Cain seems to mock God's feigned ignorance. Does God really not know? Who is he to tell God what's going on? After all, God had no trouble finding His way to Abel's sacrifice; He should have no trouble now that Abel *is* the sacrifice.

Cain is a man of faith. He has faith in God's omnipotence, and instead of offering an answer which could be interpreted as limiting God's capabilities, he humbly defers to answer.

Cain has a good point and it is with good reason that Cain has adopted an acerbic temperament. The last time he took a stand, by initiating an offering, his efforts were rebuffed. And when he responded by showing displeasure with God's rejection, he was told to get over it. This time around Cain knows better. Instead of presenting himself as the one deserving God's attention, he professes no dominion over his younger brother whatsoever.

One can almost hear Cain deliver his ironclad defense, "I am not my brother's keeper, You are. I tried to take charge, but You placed my brother over me, remember? Had You accepted my sacrifice and put me in charge, none of this would have ever happened".

Cain is a devout believer in divine providence, and wants to desperately understand the recent events as God's will.

Cain isn't addressing this merely on a personal level, but on a philosophical one. God asks the whereabouts of both 'Abel' (on a personal level), and 'his brother' (on a universal level). Notice how Cain objects to the role of 'brother's' keeper, not to the role of 'Abel's' keeper.

With his simple question, "am I my brother's keeper?" Cain means to exonerate all of mankind as mere mute creations, incapable of taking a stand. Whatever happens — whether our sacrifices are rejected or our fellow man is in distress — is divinely ordained, and we must accept our fates. "All is in the hands of heaven, save for the fear of heaven".[2]

Cain makes a valiant effort to deflect the blame. At first look it is a little hard to tell whether God simply ignores Cain's defense, or addresses his claims. God seems to simply throw the blame back at Cain, "What have *you* done?" Not *Me!*

It seems Cain was breaking new ground with his act of fratricide and behaved more like a butcher than an assassin. Not knowing where the soul would depart from, he resorted to making multiple stab wounds up and down Abel's body.[3] By the time he finally succeeded by slitting Abel's throat, he had riddled Abel's body with countless lacerations. Forensics would have had a field day collecting incriminating evidence... or would they?

Contrary to what would be expected, this crime scene was actually spotless. With an average of 5 liters of blood flowing through 100,000 miles of blood vessels in the human body, blood must have been spewing everywhere. But by the time the deed was done, there was not a drop to be found anywhere.[4] It seems that Cain had a very able accomplice.

God makes a special point of mentioning the ground's role in this despicable act. The ground opened its mouth wide and received his brother's blood. Is it really necessary to mention the natural phenomenon of the earth absorbing a liquid spilled on its surface? Wouldn't it have been more amazing if the blood had been refused admission into the earth's soil? The ground acts wholly within its nature without voicing an objection, instead, relying on a just God to take care of matters.

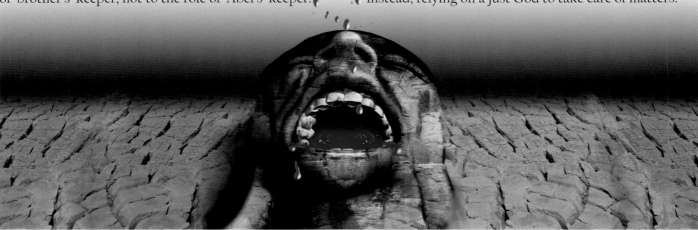

Yet, for this wholly natural act, scripture seems to hold the ground liable. In fact the Rabbis tell us that from that point on, the ground was never given permission to open its mouth for good. It was to be utilized only as an instrument of destruction.[5] Somehow the ground was expected to behave differently.

To be sure, the ground has adequate motive to aid and abet Cain. Cain is described as the "tiller of the ground",[6] while Abel shuns the ground in favor of tending the herd. When it comes time to offer a sacrifice to God, Cain elevates the ground's produce to sacred status. In return, Mother Earth does what she can to protect her favorite son.

If there is a villain to be found in the inanimate world, Abel's blood might be a more likely candidate. Abel's blood doesn't take this lying down. The blood cries out to heaven. While the ground strove to conceal, the blood does what it can to reveal. As God tells Cain, "The voice of your brother's blood cries out to Me from the ground!"[7] The blood finds a way to suspend the laws of nature, and voices its outrage. Unlike the ground, Abel's blood refuses to accept its fate. It takes exception to the 'natural' order of events. The blood's outrage may originate from the ground, but it is ultimately directed towards God. Is this not blasphemous? Such insubordination could set a dangerous precedent. Yet God hears the cries of the blood, punishes the ground, and brings justice based on those cries.

Cain can be understood as taking his cue from the ground. After all, man was created from the ground '*min-ha'adoma*'[8] and his name, '*Adom*' seems to allude to his true kinship with the ground. What Cain failed to realize is that the word '*dom*' which means blood is Adom's true heritage. Man is to take his cue, not from the '*adoma*', which is related to the word *silent*, but from the '*dom*', which the Torah refers to as 'life', "For the blood, it is the life".[9]

Abel's blood teaches us not only to renounce evil, ("your brother's blood cries out") but that the fight against evil must be waged at heaven's gates ("to Me"). By rejecting the passive, obedient ground, and accepting the rebellious insubordination of Abel's blood, God in essence has granted man the right to rebel against Him! Not only is he allowed to, but it is only through his rebellion that man truly acknowledges God's presence. As the French writer, Albert Camus writes in his work, 'The Rebel', "The metaphysical rebel ranges himself against a power whose existence he simultaneously affirms, he only admits the existence of this power at the very instant that he calls it into question".[10]

Apathy

God indeed counters Cain's defense. His opening question, "What have you *done?*" indicates God's desire for action over thought, deeds over feelings, and even rebellion over obedience. The human condition is not a blessing from God; it is a curse. As God had told Cain, "sin rests at the door. It desires you, yet you can conquer it".[11] And since this curse emanates directly from God, as King David proclaims, "You [God] turn man back until he is crushed".[12] Any act of rebellion must be unto God. King David continues in the same verse to admit that God indeed wants this act of rebellion, "and You say, 'Return, O sons of man'".[13] Furthermore, the word '*adom*' is only used by King David in the second part of the verse where man is supposed to act like the '*dom*' by rebelling, the first reference to man where he is not fighting back, but weighed down by the human condition, uses the word '*enosh*' instead.

As with any trait, rebellion must be done with restraint, "Restraint is not the contrary to revolt. Revolt carries with it the very idea of restraint ... all that remains to him is his power to rebel ... without surrendering to the arrogance of blasphemy".[14] Camus is clear that unrestrained rebellion, a rebellion without limits, ends up a tyranny. In fact the name of the most depraved city in the ancient world has its origins in unrestrained rebellion. Sodom is the word '*dom*' prefaced by the letter '*samech*' (So-dom) as opposed to the word '*Adom*' which has an '*aleph*' before the word '*dom*' (A-dom). The letter '*aleph*' represents restraint, while the '*samech*' stands for support.[15] The city of Sodom accepted no restraint. Its rebellion was complete and unmitigated.

And what form did this illicit rebellion take? The prophet Ezekiel[16] describes the horror, "Behold, this was the sin of Sodom, your sister: She and her daughters had pride, surfeit of bread and peaceful serenity, but she did not strengthen the hand of the poor and the needy".

No gas chambers or crematoria. Instead, they simply enjoyed peaceful serenity and did not regard the needy! For that they were incinerated out of existence. They emulated the ground's silence towards injustice. Their rebellion turned into a self-absorption of insane proportions.

It is no coincidence that the first example of genuine rebellion, finds *Adom* in the guise of the patriarch Abraham, in defense of the city of Sodom. When God informs Abraham of His intentions to wipe out the city, Abraham has the audacity to appear more righteous than God Himself and plead for its salvation. Not only plead, but fight! The Torah uses the word '*vayigash*' to describe Abraham's approach before God. Rashi confirms the fact

that such language indicates a highly aggressive, war-like stance. Abraham is ready to do battle with God, yet he never lost sight of his place vis-à-vis the creator of the universe. Abraham admits, "I am but dust and ash".[17] God is pleased with Abraham's resolve to fight for the Sodomites, especially in contrast to the non-confrontational approach which God encountered when He told Noah that he intended to flood the earth. Noah walked with God, but Abraham walked before God.[18]

While Abraham is the father of rebellion, it is his grandson Jacob who institutionalizes the concept for an entire nation. On the eve of the patriarch Jacob's showdown with his brother Esau, he is engaged in a battle with a heavenly entity. As a result of his great valor, God changes his name from Jacob, which alludes to his mundane struggles with his brother, to *Israel*, which appropriately enough means *he who prevailed over the Divine!*

Jacob's rebellion, like all good rebellions, could not end without the element of restraint. Before releasing the patriarch, the heavenly entity inflicts a crippling blow to Jacob's thigh. At that moment, perhaps as a constant reminder for all future rebels, God institutes the prohibition of eating the upper thigh sinew of animals.

Blood is forbidden to eat... for it is the life force, and now the symbol of restraint, in the form of a sinew, is taken off the menu.

History is replete with examples of sanctioned rebellion. All the greats from Moses to Jonah, from Rebecca to Hannah, fought the good fight.

It is most fitting that within the first murder we find the concept of rebellion. Camus goes to great lengths to contrast murder with rebellion. According to Camus, "The rebel thus rejects divinity in order to share in the struggles and destiny of all men".[19] Therefore Camus reasons, "Man's solidarity is founded upon rebellion ... any rebellion which claims the right to deny or destroy this solidarity ... becomes in reality an acquiescence in murder".[20] Hence, we find Cain's punishment for his act of murder is to live as a wanderer with a solitary life devoid of solidarity with man.

The shocking silence heard around the world as the Third Reich unleashed its atrocities, reveals man's propensity towards abject apathy. The world is content to swallow all the spilled blood in false piety. No need to cry out against injustice when all is heavenly ordained. After all, if God hadn't rejected Cain's sacrifice, none of this would have happened. This is His will, far be it for humble man to dare interfere.

When man thinks himself a god, he does not rebel against God in as much as he simply denies Him. Just as one cannot exert a force upon an object which does not exist, rebellion cannot take hold where no allegiance has been formed. Where one doubts God's very existence there is no possibility of rebelling and therefore no chance of forging a relationship.

Two nations have arisen which stand in direct opposition to each other; Israel as the chosen people and Amalek as their arch enemy for all time. This classic rivalry defines good and evil and determines right from wrong. If the Jewish people represent God's beloved and is called Israel because of their willingness to fight 'against' God, what manner of evil could exist in the hearts and minds of the 'Evil Empire', Amalek?

If Israel's rebellious nature actually aligns it with the will of God, then it would stand to reason that Amalek suffers most of all from apathy. Amalek's inability to recognize God, makes it unable to rebel and ultimately incapable of realigning with God.

Just as Israel's nature can be known by its name, so too Amalek can correlate its wickedness with its name. The numerical value of the name Amalek is 240 which is also the numerical value of the word 'safek', to doubt. Amalek, the Rabbis tell us, derives its evil from its skeptic tendencies. If the worst Amalek can do is doubt there is a God, the best we can do is be certain that there is one. When Amalek confronts the injustice inherent in the human condition he has no choice but to embrace it and eventually even emulate it; he has no other recourse. The world he inhabits is a freak of nature, to be sure; it is an anomaly, created against almost impossible odds, yet its very existence remains nothing more than natural; everything about it is 'natural'. Words like 'fair' and 'just' have no meaning in physical nature. To quote Camus one last time, "The only thing that gives meaning to human protest is the idea of a personal God who has created, and is therefore responsible for, everything".[21]

Still Life

God's creation of the universe came about by dividing elements: Order from chaos, light from dark, heaven from earth, land from sea, and so on. The first couple of days were a smashing success. But by the third day of creation, insubordination rears its ugly head. In a defiant move, we find the earth rejecting God's instructions to produce trees whose bark tastes like its fruit; opting instead to bring forth flavorless trees. The earth's rationale? If the bark tastes like the fruit, people will not wait for the fruit to ripen and they will consume the very tree itself.

This sounds like a rational idea. Perhaps it was a bold move in the right direction; was it indeed diabolical? In fact, initially the earth's modifications seem to be accepted by the Almighty. God proclaims the acts of the third day as 'good'.

The earth realized that man was an impetuous creature, and given the opportunity, he would easily squander the everlasting in favor of ephemeral gratification. The tree exists from season to season, year to year, while the fruit has its time of harvest and quickly rots away. By rendering the tree inedible, the earth focused man's attention away from the everlasting tree and squarely on the transient fruit.

The 'selections' of the Third Reich went even further than the earth's insubordination, in turning man's attention away from the eternal. In Auschwitz-Birkenau inmates who did not die on their own were systematically selected for death. These selections consisted of a senior SS officer practically arbitrarily flipping his finger right for

life, and left for death, as inmates passed before his casual gaze. My father was an inmate of Auschwitz-Birkenau at the end of 1944, where he experienced the selection process first hand. The Nazis chose the holiest days of the Jewish calendar to conduct their selections. The first was held on Rosh HaShanah, the day of judgment. The second fell on *Kol Nidre* night, the holiest night of the year. On both occasions, my father was sent to the right. By the third selection, held on Succoth, he was sent to the left. To this day, whenever he hears a diesel truck start up, he flashes back to that night, and the sound the trucks made as they carried their human cargo to the gas chambers. On the way to their deaths, some 5,000 boys in his selection sang *Ani Ma'amin/I Believe* in unison and spoke of loved ones they hoped to be reunited with in the afterlife. In my father's case he was fortunate that at the last minute a top SS officer happened to notice that a few of the boys still had some strength left in them, and pulled them from the others.

When the Nazis meted out death sentences with the wave of a finger, they robbed mankind of faith in an orderly universe. Life and death was no longer by the hand of God, but in the finger of monsters. Modern man, having witnessed this abuse of the divine domain, could come to only one conclusion: chaos and uncertainty now reign supreme.

In fact the greatest advances in modern theoretical science seem to support this theory. In physics, the Chaos Principle states that finite predictions of cause and effect are impossible to determine. In quantum physics, the Uncertainty Principle further breaks down the laws of 'cause and effect': "If we take Heisenberg's view for granted, strict causality is broken, or better: the past and future events of particles are indeterminate. One cannot calculate the precise future motion of a particle, but only a range of possibilities. Physics loses its grip. The dream of physicists, to be able to predict any future event in the universe based on its present state, meets its certain death".[1]

Although the Nazis were motivated by a sense of mockery, their choice of Succoth as the date for the final selection may actually provide a way back from the brink of total chaos. On Succoth Jews are instructed to take the *Four Species*, which consists of four different plants (which serve to represent the full community of Israel) and wave them in the air. It is within that service that Jews of faith can find a suitable counterweight to the apparent arbitrariness with which life and death were meted out in the death camps' notorious selection process. As a nation who has witnessed the power of a single finger waving back and forth, we cannot wave our *Four Species* in casualness. While reasons are given for the waving of the *Four Species*, we may find clues to its hidden secrets by analyzing a seemingly unrelated portion of the Torah.

The Jewish people read the enigmatic Book of Jonah at the close of the Day of Atonement. On the heels of that reading comes the holiday of Succoth. While the reading of Jonah certainly pertains to the theme of the Day of Atonement, there are threads of thought within Jonah that find their expression in the service of Succoth and its *Four Species*.

The prophet Jonah grapples with the indeterminate nature of reality, and struggles to exist in a seemingly unordered universe. When he is forced, not only to witness, but to serve as an instrument for, the salvation of the wicked people of the city of Nineveh, he is dumbfounded by the apparent indeterminism of God's actions. At various points in the narrative, we see Jonah moved to the point of suicide.

God defends His beneficent treatment of the wicked, with one final statement to the entire Book of Jonah: "Shall I not take pity on Nineveh the great city, in which there are more than a hundred and twenty thousand persons who do not know their right hand from their left?"[2] To this statement Jonah offers no rebuttal.

God is telling us that we will not know or understand His reasons – but He has them. There will be times when we – the observers, the victims, the heroes – will have to take His plan on faith.

In truth, even Chaos theory and the Uncertainty Principle tell us this. In Chaos theory it is not the indeterminism of an event that creates the unpredictable results, rather it is the impreciseness of human ability to adequately account for all relevant variables. Meaning: finite humans are limited in their ability to predict an outcome, but an observer with infinite capabilities can actually recognize all the contributing factors to the future outcome and testify to the determinate nature of the end result.

As far as the Uncertainty Principle goes, there, as well, it seems that inherent faults in finite measuring apparatus are the underlying cause for the erratic behavior witnessed on the subatomic level: "On subatomic scales, the photons that hit the subatomic particle will cause it to move significantly, so although the position has been measured accurately, the velocity of the particle will have been altered. By learning the position, you have rendered any information you previously had on the velocity useless. In other words, the observer affects the observed".[3] Again, it is only our inability to truly know our right from our left that creates the illusion of chaos and uncertainty.

We do not fully understand why we wave the *Four Species*, but we have no doubt that its waving has meaning. We do not understand why some were selected for life while others for death, but we have no doubt that the choice was made by the hand of providence as part of some master plan, and not the finger of evil, trying to create the master race.

The Rabbis tell us that there is one tree which defied the earth's alteration, and indeed its bark mimicked the taste of its fruit. The Citron emulates God's original intent.

It is this fruit that we bundle with the three other species to form the *Four Species*; which we then wave on

Succoth. Its value is not in what it does, but what it *is*. On the holiday, it is forbidden to even smell the fruit, because it is designated for a higher purpose. The Citron achieves its potential, not in feeding the poor, or as an elixir curing the ill, but in simply being.

The Citron brings our focus back to the everlasting. In fact, the Tree of Life, which s t o o d with the Tree of Knowledge in the Garden of Eden, also had delicious bark, but it is not what it had that matters as much as what it lacked — the Tree of Life bore no fruit at all!

In Nineveh the salvation of the wicked, who did not know their left from their right, pushed a man of God to the brink of his existence. In the concentration camps of the Third Reich, the demise of the righteous, which were brutally taught their right from their left, brought the people of God to the brink of their existence.

When we wave the Four Species in all six directions, we make sure to return to center. This way, amid all the elaborate waving, which forces the Four Species to point and shake, to bend and shutter, they invariably return, recompose and remain — perfectly straight.

Ignorance indeed is bliss; to know is madness. God had mercy on Nineveh and its inhabitants, who lived in bliss, completely oblivious to the wild misdirections life threw their way. All the more so, may God have mercy upon us. We stand forever burdened with more knowledge than we ever hoped for — an uncanny sense of direction which only serves to disorient, confuse and confound us; for only those who know where they are going can truly be considered lost.

Sticks & Stacks

"She tastes that her merchandise is good, her candle does not go out at night".
Proverbs 31:18 Aishet Chayil

Judaism seems to be locked in a constant downward spiral. Every generation seems to fall short of its predecessor, both in spirit as well as in deeds. The phrase in Rabbinic literature is, *Hitkatnu hadorot/ generational degeneration*. While Darwin's *Evolution* sees physical organisms racing towards greater and greater levels of perfection, Judaism acknowledges a palpable spiritual weakening.

In physics, Newton's third law teaches us that every action has an equal and opposite reaction. It seems the same concept holds true in the spiritual world. As we weaken, so does God's manifestation. As it says in the Torah, "you behave casually with Me, then I, too, will behave toward you with casualness..."[1] Unfortunately the verse does not end there. It goes on to say "...and I will strike you".[2]

The light of open miracles, prophets, and oracles has been blotted out by pogroms, long exiles, and concentration camps. "The Eternal shall smite thee with madness, and blindness, and disquietude of heart: And thou shalt grope at noon-day, as the blind gropeth in thick darkness".[3] It is bad enough that we exist in a thick darkness, but what is worse is that our spiritual vision is without night-vision, sonar, or radar.

Reb Shlomo HaCohen of Radomsk, comments, "That even though our merits are diminished as compared to previous generations, God looks upon us with favor, and He accepts our meager efforts willingly and with love".

Reb Shlomo likens the condition to a complicated legal provision called, '*Tam k'Iykar*'. The law states that the mere taste of a forbidden food is enough to render the entire dish unkosher. In the absence of substance, a mere taste will suffice. "In earlier years, the *Mitzvot* and the Torah of our people was notable both in substance and in impact. Their thoughts, their hearts and their actions all contributed to a significant service of God. Now, after many punishing years in the exile, which is compared to darkness, our people continue to be dispersed, and it seems that all we can do is to contribute a 'taste' of a true service of God".

It is that taste that King Solomon speaks of when he praises Jewish mothers and daughters in the portion of Proverbs sung every Friday night as '*Aishet Chayil*': "She tastes that her merchandise is good, her candle does not go out at night".[4] It may be dark and our vision weak, but the women of the Jewish people light up the night and disperse great amounts of darkness in their simple faith that their candlesticks can outshine the grotesque chimney stacks of the crematoria. While it is our candles that burn, it is their chimneys that melt away.

Still Life

Lullaby

Often the first words a Jewish child is taught, and the last prayer on the lips of a Jew before his soul departs, is the proclamation of his unwavering belief in one God.[1] The six Hebrew words of the *Shema* serve as that declaration of faith: *Shema Yisrael, Hashem Elokenu, Hashem echad/Hear O Israel, the Lord is our God, the Lord is one.* It is the first commandment a Jew must perform when he turns *Bar Mitzvah* at the age of 13 and it is the topic of the first discussion in the Oral Law. The *Shema* is the only prayer the Jew offers which requires so much concentration that he is instructed to cover his eyes while uttering its six words. Yet, in spite of the *Shema's* lofty stature, it is rather commonplace. It is to be found on the lips of observant Jews at least three times a day.

The question becomes: should there be such a mingling of the sacrosanct and the mundane in man's actions? Can six words be so extraordinary on the one hand and so ubiquitous on the other? Should I be freely allowed to utter the same declaration as a young mother being gassed to death while holding her infant child?

How dare I?

Yet my earliest memories are of my father putting me to bed by placing my hand on the *mezuzah* on my room's door-post, covering my eyes, and there, teaching me to recite the *Shema*. His own mother was gassed to death with two of her young children; now he entrusts me with the incantation that was most likely her last words?

There is a counter-intuitive concept in Jewish law which just may serve to grant me the permission I seek. The Law states that when there is a conflict between two actions, the action which is performed more often takes precedence.[2] This hierarchy is not simply a pecking order, but a concept rooted deep within Jewish thought. Judaism is not a religion of transcendence, where the goal is to achieve some elevated state of nirvana. There is no ascetic or monastic retreat for the Jew; no manner of escape or refuge to altered states. Instead, Judaism takes up residence squarely within reality. Its 613 commandments focus the Jew's devotion on the task at hand rather than a world to come.

What the law of the 'commonplace' (*tadir*) may be teaching us is that our natural tendency to look for a supernatural revelation as the apex of religious experience is out of focus. The real experience of the transcendental is in the everyday act. Commenting on the emphasis placed by King Solomon in Ecclesiastes, on the passage of time, "to everything there is a season",[3] the philosopher Søren Kierkegaard points out that, "If there is, then, something eternal in a man, it must be able to exist and to be grasped

within every change".[4] Meaning, that while King Solomon delegates earthly matters to specific times in a person's life — "He has set eternity within man's heart".[5] The eternal is accessible at all times. Every present moment is a manifestation of the everlasting. It is, most of all, in the repetitive movements we perform every day where we meet and embrace the Divine.

Professor Yeshayahu Leibowitz was perhaps the strongest proponent for Judaism's attraction to, if not obsession with, the mundane and the monotonous. Professor Leibowitz unabashedly presents a picture of Judaism wherein the spiritual has very little to do with the spirit. "The fundamental and enduring elements of human existence are in life's prose, not in its poetry. The Judaism of the *Halakhah* despises rhetoric, avoids pathos, abjures the visionary. Above all, it rejects the illusory. It does not permit a man to believe that the conditions of his existence are other than they really are. It prevents flight from one's functions and tasks in this inferior world to an imaginary world which is all good, beautiful, and sublime".[6]

Four kings rose up in Israel and displayed varied degrees of faith in the creator: King David, Asa, Jehoshaphat, and Hezekiah. David asked God to allow him to pursue and overtake his enemy. Asa asked God to allow him to pursue his enemy; however he requested they be overtaken by God Himself. For Jehoshaphat even the pursuit was too much, and he offered songs of praise in exchange for God's intervention in both pursuing as well as overtaking his enemy. And Hezekiah had strength neither to overcome, pursue, or even offer praise, he left his fate completely in God's hands. All four kings were successful but when Hezekiah was able to completely extricate himself from any participation whatsoever, God desired to make Hezekiah the Messiah!

Hezekiah's heroism was spectacular and earned him a spot among the greatest monarchs ever to rule, but his act of faith was in fact the lowest among the four. King David and his desire to act in the name of God was preferred over all the other kings with their less-than-participatory modes of interaction. David's ability to engage fully in the minutia of battle and involve himself directly with the acts of war was the purest expression of faith. The greatest sanctification of God's name comes about, not through *His* miraculous ways, but through *our* extraordinary efforts.

In Kabbalistic teachings, there is a concept of 'Contraction'. Rav Soloveitchik uses a form of this concept to describe the way finite man can make the existential leap towards the infinite. According to Rav Solovetchik, we don't in fact leap toward the infinite; rather the infinite is released within the finite. In a way, man, from within his temporal world, brings God and the infinite to life. In this way the material world does not stand in contradiction to the everlasting, it serves as a vehicle for its realization.

That is why Judaism is a religion rooted in action. It is through our actions in a physical world that we touch the spiritual presence of God. God proclaims, "They shall make for Me a sanctuary – so that I may dwell among them".[7] We are not exhorted to purify ourselves in order to reach God. Rather the goal, as described by God Himself, is for Him to dwell among us.

According to this line of reasoning, it is the daily recitation of the *Shema* which gives it its holiness. While a single occurrence can mark an impressive display of faith,

it is the repeated answering of the question day in and day out that stands as the true test of the believer. It is the fact that my grandmother taught my father to say the *Shema* three times a day, and that he taught me to do the same, which infuses those six words with the holiness befitting a mother's last breath.

While the six words of the *Shema* have sufficed throughout the ages, the *Shema* my father taught me did have a postscript. I don't suppose he made up the addendum, but it was certainly appropriate coming from his lips. The words; *Shadai, yishmarayni, umazelayni, mekol rah,* followed the standard *Shema* and was his legacy to the post-Holocaust generations. "God, guard over me, and save me, from all evil".

The Sound of Sacrifice

When all else fails and words lose their meaning, when the human condition renders us not just speechless, but utterly mute, even beyond tears, we can only turn to the primordial scream of the ram's horn to say the unsayable. We take comfort in knowing that our inarticulacy is not the end of the line.

In fact, after 149 Psalms, composed by King David, where he expounds every manner of praise toward the Creator, his final Psalm finds its expression in the wordless — the music of instruments without lyrics. Rav Moshe Eisemann makes this point in his book, '*Music Made in Heaven*', and quotes Rav Soloveitchik as seeing in this, "that the most inspired words must inevitably fall short of what really needs to be said".[1]

While it is relatively easy to see how musical instruments can bring one spiritual expression, the ram's horn is not known for its melodic properties. Why make *it* the instrument of choice?

Rav Abbahu said, "Why do we blow a ram's horn? The Holy One, Blessed Be He, said: 'Sound before Me a ram's horn so that I may remember on your behalf the binding of Isaac the son of Abraham, and account it to you as if you had bound yourselves before Me'".[2]

It is the associative qualities inherent in the ram's horn which earn it a central role in our communicative repertoire. The incident which propels the ram's horn to religious prominence is the binding of Isaac. Throughout the ages this story has attracted the greatest thinkers. Most notably, the philosopher Søren Kierkegaard, in his work '*Fear and Trembling*', discusses *the binding* as the epitome of faith. Kierkegaard maintains that the

greatness of Abraham, and the reason he is the father of faith, is because he was capable of performing the sacrifice without making a sacrifice. Abraham was able to take a leap of faith. He held fast to the notion that somehow the impossible could happen; he could offer Issac and still keep Isaac. Abraham could in essence have his cake and eat it too.

During Abraham's times, human sacrifice was a widespread custom; the idea of a father slaughtering his son on the altar was not altogether uncommon. Kierkegaard makes the point that unless we invest Abraham with his *leap of faith* theory, we might as well consider Abraham no less, and no more, than a cold-blooded murderer!

Kierkegaard contends that even he could perform the motions of the sacrifice, but he would never be able to offer the sacrifice as a leap beyond human reason the way Abraham did. In which case, his sacrifice would be just that: a full-fledged sacrifice of everything he holds dear — a resignation that all is lost. Average man is capable of such a sacrifice. Give it all up for God. Abraham however, was able to simultaneously offer all he has, and yet expect, somehow, to get it all back. He resisted the path of less resistance, which would have been that of resignation, in favor of a suspension of finite reality. Abraham's faith was pure, and what would seem absurd to all others was the norm to such a man of faith. That is why Abraham failed to tell his wife Sarah of his intentions to offer their son. He knew that what he was performing was beyond the realm of accepted behavior.

Kierkegaard presents a powerful portrayal, but is it powerful enough? Modern man has witnessed six million such sacrifices, does the ancient story still resonate with value? Must our post-Holocaust generation supplant Søren Kierkegaard with the likes of Bob Dylan?

In his 1965 ballad, Highway 61 Revisited, Dylan puts faith to rest, and gives rise to doubt and arbitrariness.

> *Oh God said to Abraham, "Kill me a son".*
> *Abe says, "Man, you must be puttin' me on".*
> *God says, "No". Abe say, "What?"*
> *God says, "You can do what you want Abe, but the next time you*
> *see me comin' you better run".*
> *Well Abe says, "Where do you want this killin' done?"*
> *God says, "Out on Highway 61".[3]*

Dylan's God seems to capriciously decide he needs a *killin* done. And when Abe inquires as to where this *killin* should be done — as if to say, there must be a point to all this — God adds insult to injury by denying Abe any meaning. Just go out on Highway 61.

How can the ram's horn continue to communicate on our behalf? Is there a way around Dylan's cynicism? Or are we destined to thumb a ride down a four-lane highway, not caring in which direction we head?

A decade before Dylan reduced man's faith to an accident out on highway 61, the French writer Albert Camus began unraveling Kierkegaard's leap of faith. Camus contended, "This leap is an escape".[4] "The leap doesn't represent an extreme danger [the ultimate goal in life] as Kierkegaard would like it to do. The danger, on the contrary, lies in the subtle instant that precedes the leap. Being able to remain on that dizzying crest – that is integrity and the rest is subterfuge".[5]

Basically, life is the contradiction "between the mind that desires and the world that disappoints".[6] "Living is keeping the absurd alive".[7] Man lives suspended between his quest for understanding and his inability to comprehend. If you do away with either the quest or the inability to satisfy that quest, you render life impotent. When Kierkegaard speaks of a leap, he takes away our striving to understand, he disarms our intellect, for "The entire effort of his intelligence is to escape the antinomy of the human condition".[8]

The Torah's blatant omission of an afterlife seems to support Camus's *suspended leap.*

There is no room for solving the dilemma that is life, by putting our hope in another life. Rav Soloveitchik puts the ball squarely in our court, "It is this world which constitutes the stage for the Law, the setting for (*halakhic*) man's life. It is here that the Law can be implemented to a greater or lesser degree. It is here that it can pass from potentiality into actuality. It is here, in this world, that (*halakhic*) man acquires eternal life!"[9]

Rav Soloveitchik is clearly siding with Camus. The Rav continues, "The religious experience, from beginning to end, is antinomic and antithetic ... Religion is not, at the outset, a refuge of grace and mercy for the despondent and desperate, an enchanted stream for crushed spirits, but a raging, clamorous torrent of man's consciousness with all its crises, pangs, and torments".[10]

There is one phrase in the Torah which speaks directly to our topic. It is so revealing that when the Jewish people uttered it, God proclaimed, "Who revealed this secret to my children?! This is the secret of the heavenly ministering angels!"[11] When God asks the Jewish people if they want to receive the Torah they answer, "Everything that God says, we will do and we will hear (*Na'aseh VeNishma*)!"[12]

The spectacular positioning of the action before the understanding is crucial to our discussion. What they were expressing was a clear understanding of the human condition. Between the words *Na'aseh* and *Nishma* there is the letter 'vav'. That letter is where existence resides. Man must remain in a state of constant flux between his finite actions and his inability to fathom their infinite consequences.

The *Midrash*[13] gives us a glimpse into Abraham's state of mind throughout the drama, and it too beckons us away from Kierkegaard's leap. The *Midrash* acknowledges the confusion God built into the dynamics of this event. "Abraham arose and asked: Yesterday You [God] told me "For in Isaac shall seed be called to thee",[14] and today You told me "Take now, thy son, thine only son ... and offer him there for a burnt-offering".[15] It seemed to Abraham as if the words of God were contradictory, nevertheless, he overcame the pangs and torments of contradiction, rose up early and saddled his donkey.[16]

God deliberately placed the patriarch in total confusion. Abraham was willing to face down his insecurities and doubts and proceed as a man of action.

Therein lies faith! Abraham did not resort to postulating some irrational conclusion, as Kierkegaard proposes; instead he embraced his role as a finite being in a relationship with the infinite. He made no attempt to reconcile. The 'Na'aseh' must occur while the 'Nishma' is still at bay. Man must strive for understanding yet realize he never will understand.

Life indeed takes place on Highway 61.

When the angel puts an end to Abraham's attempted sacrifice, it directs him to a thicket wherein a ram is struggling to free itself from the entangled branches. "And Abraham lifted up his eyes and looked and behold,

behind him a ram caught in the thicket by its horns".[17] "This teaches that the Holy One, Blessed be He, showed our father Abraham the ram tearing itself free from one thicket and getting entangled in another. The Holy One, Blessed be He, said to Abraham: 'In a similar manner are your children destined to be caught up in iniquities and entangled in troubles, but they will ultimately be redeemed through the horns of the ram'".[18]

This is what gives the ram's horn its special quality. It is a signpost directing our attention to the reality of life. Our inability to fully comprehend the world we live in is a natural component of the human condition, as is our desire to continue to seek explanations. The ram's horn both heralds and wails.

Cosmic Ash

After days, if not weeks, spent in a prolonged state of suffocation, starvation and dehydration, many succumbed. Those who survived ultimately reached their journey's end, which would be the final destination for most. When the huge doors of the cattle cars were pried open air flooded into the vacuous void trying its best to revive those still strong enough to gasp. However, the air could do little to disperse the stench and noxious fumes.

Upon arriving at Auschwitz-Birkenau, my grandfather, Dov Lebovic, a Czechoslovakian veteran of World War I, turned to his sons and warned them that the odor in the air was unmistakably that of burning human flesh. It was a smell he experienced in the first Great War.

It was no secret that the huge chimneys, which roared day and night, ablaze in orange flames, spewing black smoke and sending grey ash off into the heavens were incinerating arrivals from previous transports. The smell of death was overpowering. Historians estimate that in a single day at Auschwitz-Birkenau, 20,000 victims were reduced to ash.

When the Jewish patriarch, Jacob, traverses the Yabuk River to rescue a forsaken vessel, he meets a

formidable foe. Rabbinic commentators recognize this foe as none other than the angel of Jacob's twin, Esau. Esau and Jacob are destined to be archenemies and wage war throughout the ages. The Talmud[1] references a descendant of Esau called Germamia. Rav Yaakov Emden, who lived in the 18th century, identified this nation as none other than — the German people. Hence, when we read about Jacob clenched in battle throughout a long dark night along the Yabuk, we can perhaps recognize the scene in its twentieth century setting on the Rhine.

In this foreshadowing incident, scripture records a seemingly incidental detail, upon which the sages elaborate. The Torah makes mention of the dust beneath the warriors' feet. It is said that the dust produced from the shifting earth beneath their battle encircled them and rose into the atmosphere until it reached the throne of God Himself.[2] It was only once the dust and ash had reached the Heavenly Throne, that Jacob could be declared the victor, and have his name changed to Israel.

The import of mere dust floating heavenward seems to add little to the narrative concerning the patriarch and his nemesis. However, fast-forward to the modern day confrontation between Jacob and Esau, and the sanctification of dust and ash is most appropriate. For it is upon the merit of those cremated souls, whose remains rose from the chimneys till they reached the heavens, that Israel emerged victorious.

Indeed, in a macabre gesture — ironically fitting — Adolf Eichmann, the logistics supervisor for the mass exterminations, posted a sign above the crematorium at Birkenau: "This is the gate of the Lord into which the righteous will enter".[3]

The victims of the Holocaust inhabit a place in the spiritual world unattainable by saints and inaccessible even to angels.

On Holy Ground

The Torah offers us a front row seat at the monumental first encounter between God and His most accomplished servant, Moses. Every detail of this moment holds fascinating insights into the nature of our relationship with the Creator. Specifically as it relates to suffering and survival, this maiden rendezvous speaks volumes to our post-Holocaust existence.

The first stop, relevant to our search for metaphysical themes, can be found within the very description of the miraculous event itself. God chooses to speak to Moses from the lowly branches of a desert thorn bush. Controversy over the condition of the bush raises some intriguing concepts. When the Torah describes the incendiary apparition, it declares, "He, (Moses) saw and behold! The bush was burning in the fire but the bush was not consumed".[1] Yet when Moses himself describes his bewilderment, it is not directed towards a burning bush, rather, he sees an unscathed, bush. Not only is it not consumed, but it is not even showing signs of damage. As it states, "Moses thought, ... 'Why will the bush not be burned?'"[2]

Whether the bush was scorched by flames or merely engulfed in them, the commentators push the notion that the tiny thorn bush represents the Jewish people, and the flames allude to pain and suffering. It is from within that pain and suffering, in between thorn and thistle, that God becomes manifest.

When it comes to suffering, there is a classic divergence in the Talmud between the great sage Rabbi Nachum Ish Gamzu and his prized student, Rabbi Akiva. Nachum Ish Gamzu was known for his philosophy of, 'this too (*Gam Zu*) is for the best'.[3] While Rabbi Akiva's dictum in life was, 'all is for the best'.[4] The two phrases are similar enough to excuse confusing them as identical. In reality, they express outlooks on life which lie at opposite ends of the spectrum. You might say: while one glows the other burns.

A closer look: In the morning prayers, a verse from Isaiah is intentionally misquoted. The original phrase is "[I (God) am the One] Who makes peace and creates evil".[5] In the prayer service, the word *evil* is changed to the word:

all! Conversely, when Rabbi Akiva uses the word *all*, he clearly is referring to *evil*. He is in fact saying evil is for the best. In Rabbi Akiva's world view, there is room for such a concept as a 'necessary evil'. Ultimately all evil leads to an overall *happy ending*. But there is no getting around the existence of scorching flames with lasting scars. Rabbi Akiva's bush indeed burned. The miracle is that it would withstand the trauma and refuse to be consumed.

For Nachum Ish Gamzu, however, there is only the warm glow of God's benevolence. The bush only appeared to be in dire straits, but upon a second look, Moses could see that from twig to trunk all was safe from harm.

The difference between Rabbi Akiva and Nachum Ish Gamzu may seem slight, and on the surface, merely a couple shades of grey apart. However, in reality their positions stem from deeply divergent philosophical roots.

In his seminal work 'Fear and Trembling', Søren Kierkegaard, the great Danish philosopher, artfully delineates the two sides of this debate and adapts it to Abraham's sacrifice of his son, Isaac. His theory is that there are two types of 'faithful'. There is the Knight of Faith and the Knight of Resignation. The Knight of Faith resembles Nachum Ish Gamzu. Such an individual can face down any circumstance armed with the confidence that no evil can befall man. In the presence of impending doom, he can rely on a leap of faith to help him maintain his unrealistic outlook. For Kierkegaard, faith begins where logic ends.

The Knight of Resignation, on the other hand, is noble to be sure, but he merely accepts his fate, and does not move to transcend it. Kierkegaard himself admits that he could act as the Knight of Resignation, and sacrifice all he had to God. But a sacrifice it would certainly be. By contrast, Abraham was able to offer Isaac upon the altar without the slightest sensation of sacrifice. Kiekegaard describes Abraham in terms that would render him the quintessential proponent of *Gamzuism*. Along the lines of Nachum Ish Gamzu, Abraham could accept no evil from the Creator. He *knew* he would come out of this situation completely unscathed. Somehow God would accept his son as an offering without taking Isaac away from him. As

Abraham foretells in the narrative when instructing his servants to wait for them, "we will worship, and we [both Isaac and I] will return to you".[6]

In Kierkegaard's terminology, Rabbi Akiva would then be a Knight of Resignation, and be operating on a lower level than Nachum Ish Gamzu. Most traditional commentators would agree, according Nachum Ish Gamzu's position the higher ground. However, in the essay titled, 'The Sound of Sacrifice', which appears in this collection, we actually explore this notion of Kierkegaard's, and find his stance on faith to be a stumble rather than a leap.[7]

The strongest argument against Kierkegaard's hierarchy of Knights, comes from the French writer Albert Camus. He sees a greater strength in avoiding the crutch of a leap of faith and existing within the absurdity of the here and now. For Camus, it is the ability to remain lucid in the face of horror which demands the most in man. By denying the existence of horror, we render 'life' impotent. A more detailed discussion is outlined in 'The Sound of Sacrifice', but what is clear is that in matters of faith, the smallest divergences can ultimately create the most massive of chasms. Therefore, when we look at the burning bush as a paradigm of the philosophy of suffering, we must pay close attention to even the smallest nuances.

When the Torah initially describes the burning bush as actually burning, it is adopting Rabbi Akiva's outlook on life. When the Torah informs us that the bush burned, but refused to yield, in accordance with Rabbi Akiva's concept of evil, we are presented with the raw reality of the human condition. As Rabbi Joseph B. Soloveitchik mentions on numerous occasions, the religious life is not one of comfort and ease, but of conflict and inner struggle. When the finite confronts the infinite there will be friction. However, there will also be salvation. Ultimately all is for the good.

What Moses expressed, as his perceived reality, was a more palatable manifestation of divine rule, in line with Nachum Ish Gamzu. After all, it would be his duty to sell this new relationship to the Jewish people. A people who, much like the Holocaust generation, had endured the most oppressive of conditions. Their hearts yearned for salvation from suffering, not the mention of a suffering that brings salvation. Therefore, Moses refused the initial message of a burning bush representing a punitive God, in favor of a glowing bush more in line with a redeeming father. The words, "I will turn aside now and look at this great sight".[8] can be understood as the moment where Moses strives to soften God's image. Moses is not turning aside physically, but metaphysically. One does not usually

'turn aside' in order to 'take a look'. Moses's intent is to view the human condition from a different vantage point, and again this is not a search for a closer look, but a deeper one.

Moses is telling God that there is another way to understand pain and suffering. Moses will turn aside from the initial perception, and take the long view of history. It is true that the flames are burning the bush, but when all is said and done, and the flames subside, the bush will no longer be burned. Moses is able to shift his focus from the present to the future, and gain the benefit of interpreting current events in their historical context.

Even Moses's terminology reflects this shift in tenses, "why *will* the bush not be burned?" He cannot really deny the fact that at present it is burning, rather he can assert that with hindsight the bush will not be burned.

The question remains: Did the bush burn? Was the Egyptian exile an iron crucible where a nation was forged, or an incubator where a people were nourished? Did the extermination of six-million Jews preserve or punish God's chosen people?

There are few who could argue with the legendary Chazon Ish, and he seems to also back our Knight of Resignation, Rabbi Akiva. In his work entitled, '*Emuna u'Bitachon*', he makes the point that the view of faith that supports the concept that everything that happens to an individual is good, is incorrect. Rather, things happen that may not be good.

The Talmud in *Brachos* 60b takes on this question by discussing the requirement for man to bless God for both, the good that befalls him, as well as the evil. In that discussion Rabbi Akiva's position is granted legitimacy, but strangely enough, no mention is made of his Rabbi, Nachum Ish Gamzu. As a result, the law actually seems to side with Rabbi Akiva; for the blessing made on good fortune is different from that made on the advent of evil. One would expect Nachum Ish Gamzu to recommend a single blessing cover both occurrences since they are, in reality, both good. While Rabbi Akiva's ruling carries the day, the Rabbi's give the nod to Nachum Ish Gamzu in the Messianic era. For in that era it says that we will indeed make the same blessing on evil as we make on good. Again, the bush may burn, but it will not be burned.

In a relevant episode,[9] we find Rabbi Akiva approaching the destroyed Temple Mount and, upon seeing a jackal running through the Holy of Holies, breaking out in laughter. His companions, on the other hand, are reduced to tears. Upon hearing Rabbi Akiva's outburst, his companions question his reaction. Rabbi Akiva explains that it is his understanding that the ultimate redemption will come on the heels of utter desolation. Therefore the heinous sight of the holiest terrestrial location being trampled by a jackal, is a stark reminder that indeed utter desolation has occurred, and the redemption can begin to take hold. The source of Rabbi Akiva's laughter, is not due to the fact that a jackal running rampant in place of the high priest is a good thing to behold, his laughter stems from his acknowledgement that from the bad the good will sprout.

How would Nachum Ish Gamzu have reacted upon witnessing the renegade jackal? Would he have cried like the other disciples, or laughed along with Rabbi Akiva? I propose he'd have done neither. Crying would be out of the question because he is incapable of interpreting events in a negative light. He also would not laugh, because laughter, as understood by the philosopher John Morreall has its biological origins as a kind of shared expression of relief at the passing of danger. This theory clearly describes Rabbi Akiva's opinion. Seeing the jackal ensures an end to the current destruction and heralds a redemptive future. But for Nachum Ish Gamzu, there is no need for relief, because there never was any 'real' danger in the first place.

Moses exhibits great tenacity in this first meeting with the Creator. In addition to refusing God's initial message in favor of a more 'Gamzuistic' approach, he also determines that when revealing God's name to the people, less is more. When God tells Moses that His name is, "I Shall Be As I Shall Be".[10] He is hinting at the fact that just as He is the nation's God in this current calamity of slavery, He will be there for them throughout the many future calamities destined to be experienced by the Jewish people. However within the same verse, God drops the latter half of His name and is to be known simply as, "I Shall Be". Rashi, quoting the Talmud,[11] explains that Moses refused to bombard the fragile people with any hint of future suffering. Moses will introduce the people to their God: their 'Savior' — period. Any introductions to their God: their 'Oppressor', will have to wait.

Unfortunately future sufferings were inevitable. In our most recent brush with total annihilation, an eerie symbol provides an uncomfortable link back to the thorn bush.

The Nazis were exceedingly orderly, and maintained warehouses of artifacts left over from their millions of victims. One such stockpile which evokes visceral emotions are the piles upon piles of shoes. At the peak of the gassings, one day's collection would amount to about twenty-five thousand pairs!

In Moses's encounter, God commands him not to approach the bush, and to remove his shoes. "He [God] said, 'Do not come closer to here, remove your shoes from your feet, for the place upon which you stand is holy ground'".[12] The Torah is replete with references to shoes. Shoes play a central role in the Biblical *Chalitzah* rite (Deut. 25:5-11); in the Book of Ruth, 3:8; in the laws of *Yom Kippur*, *Tishah B'Av*, and mourning. See also Gen. 37:28: After Joseph's brothers sold him for 20 pieces of silver, they used the coins (according to various *Midrashim*) to buy shoes for themselves — a fact alluded to by Amos 2:6: "They sold the righteous for silver, and the poor one for a pair of shoes".

According to Rav Eliyahu Dessler, the wearing of shoes elevates a man above the animals, and separates him from his lowly origins of dust and earth. The shoe of the Torah, of course, is made from the skin of an animal.[13] When man wears the skin of an animal upon his feet, when he treads upon the earth by utilizing animal leather, he demonstrates that he is not just another animal. Instead, he is superior to and has the power to dominate the animal.

By instructing Moses to remove his shoes due to the fact that the ground beneath his feet is holy, God is telling Moses that whenever man finds himself engulfed in the flames of suffering, he must not allow himself to wallow in desolation. He must not succumb to the nagging question: Where is God? Instead, we must be comforted in a curious way, because suffering is always experienced on holy ground and in close proximity to the ineffable.

Inside the holiest chamber of Jerusalem's first Temple, there existed the likeness of two angels. These two stand atop the Ark. It is said that when God is happy with the Jewish people, the angels face each other in an embrace. When He is angry, the angels turn away from each other. When the temple was destroyed by the Babylonian invaders, they carried out the angels, and low-and-behold, the angels were clenched in a full embrace.[14] In the essay entitled, 'Confine, Refine, Define', we explore more closely the nature of this seemingly nefarious relationship.

Since the wearing of shoes stands as a reminder to man of his elevated status among God's creations, we are careful to remove our shoes while performing a holy act. There is no room for pride before the King of Kings. When the priests offered the sacrifices in the Holy Temple, they were barefoot. It stands to reasons that when God's holy people are offered as sacrifices, they too be barefoot!

Bloodshot

According to the Biblical commandment, the corners of a four-cornered garment must be breached : *Tzitzit*. Long threads, extending beyond the confines of the corner's right angle, are entangled for a duration by a series of knots and twines, eventually releasing their grip, setting the threads free — unencumbered.

One of the threads is dyed with the blood of an animal. The color of this dye, called *techelet*, turns out to be quite elusive. According to the Talmud it resembles the sea, which resembles the heavens, which resembles the Holy Throne of God.[1] Notice that the Talmud does not say it is similar to the *color* of the sea, rather that it resembles the sea itself. This seems no specific shade, but an impression of the vast pallet of blues and greens that paint the seas of the world. This mysterious hue, which resides at the far end of the color spectrum, conjures up the most elaborate visual landscape imaginable. *Techelet* seems to represent a demarcation of sorts. It establishes a boundary between us and God. By reminding us of what stands between us, (the vast sea and the expansive heavens) it emphasizes distance, not our direct connection to God. Seen in this light, *techelet* serves as a blemish of sorts rather than a mark of glory; yet this is the focal point of the commandment to wear *tzitzit*.

The Talmud tells us that the Jewish people were given the commandment of *techelet* because of the utterance of one word by the patriarch Abraham. Upon emerging victorious in his battle with the five kings, Abraham declines to take even a single 'thread' in spite of a generous offer of recompense by the King of Sodom. "Abram said to the king of Sodom: 'I lift up my hand to *Hashem*, God, the Most High, Maker of heaven and earth, if so much as a thread to a shoelace; or if I shall take from anything of yours!'"[2] Abraham denied himself any gain whatsoever, down to a thread and a shoelace. For this act of restraint Abraham's all white *tzitzit* are given a splash of color: *techelet*. The lone dyed thread encapsulates the humble trait Abraham exhibited by refusing to advance his own interests.

On one level the thread of *techelet* seems an appropriate reward for such behavior. Abraham restrained himself from any selfish motivation whatsoever, and denied himself even a thread, so God turned a simple thread into a commandment. On a spiritual level the connection is not as plain to see. The Talmud itself questions the logic of this compensation, essentially asking, "What good is a colored thread? The Talmud resorts to a somewhat cryptic explanation. "Reb Meir says, What distinguishes the color of *techelet* from all other colors? It resembles the sea, which resembles the sky, which resembles the throne of God".[3] The Talmud ends there, leaving us the arduous task of tying it all together.

We aren't the first to be baffled by this commandment. Even prior to the Talmud, the Torah records major confusion over the significance of *techelet*. As the Jews wandered in the desert under the able guidance of Moses, Moses's own cousin, Korach, stages a rebellion against him. Deciding that Moses has taken things too far, and the people deserve direct access to God, Korach seeks to discredit Moses's role as leader. To support his claim, Korach fashions a four-cornered garment whose entirety is dyed in *techelet*. Korach reasoned that while a single dyed thread is capable of redeeming an ordinary garment, such a thread is unnecessary where the garment itself is worthy of redemption on its own. Similarly, if the Jewish people are all 'a holy nation' there is no need for a mediator.

Korach presents the garment to Moses and demands a ruling as to whether such a garment would still require *tzitzit*. If Moses requires an all *techelet* garment be adorned with *tzitzit*, he will open himself up to criticism by defying common sense. If he agrees with Korach's viewpoint, he will be admitting his own obsolescence.

Moses is undaunted and informs his cousin that indeed the garment still would require fringes. Korach sees the inconsistency in such a ruling and presents his mutiny before the people. Instead of attempting to settle the argument himself, Moses seeks heavenly assistance. He opts for a decisive end to the matter rather than a healthy debate. God sides with Moses and swallows the rebellion in a massive earthquake.

Korach may have perished, but his logic remains intact. With such an abrupt end to the controversy, God clearly sided with Moses, but the matter is far from resolved. When the Talmud questions the value of *techelet*, it in essence resurrects Korach's argument.

Along with the unsatisfactory conclusion, the Korach saga actually shrouds its beginnings in obscurity as well. The episode of Korach's rebellion is introduced with the words, "Korach took ...",[4] but it fails to tell us what he took. We have no idea where Korach took his philosophy from, nor what doomed it. Perhaps the story does not begin with Korach. Instead Korach is taking his cue from an ancient ancestor.

The circumstances we are faced with in Korach's rebellion are eerily reminiscent of the battle between Cain and Abel. In that confrontation, its end is shrouded in obscurity. The Torah tells us that, right before killing his brother, "Cain spoke with his brother Abel",[5] but it fails to tell us what was said. Could the two stories actually be interdependent?

An overlapping reading of the two stories may bring clarity to much of our confusion. *[In Genesis]* Cain feels rejected by God when his brother's sacrifice is chosen over his. God reassures him that he too can enjoy favored status if he so chooses. *[Flash forward to Deuteronomy and]* Korach takes God's advice and presents his adversary with a proposition. *[Back to Genesis]* Cain says to his dear brother that God wants an egalitarian relationship with mankind, and the two brothers should interact equally with their Creator. *[Return to Deuteronomy and]* Moses doesn't dignify Korach's suggestion with a response based on the merits of the argument. *[In Genesis]* This infuriates Cain and leads him to murder. The ground plays a supporting role in this act of fratricide, and is employed in the later story to exact the necessary retribution. In punishing Cain, God gives Cain a sign and says He will delay retribution. When Moses prays to God to bring that retribution, God rightfully employs the ground to redeem its earlier transgression of swallowing Abel's blood by opening its mouth one more time, and swallowing the rebels alive.

If there is any doubt that these two stories are related, the 16th century *Kabbalist*, Rabbi Yitzchak Luria, reveals an even stronger connection between these incidents. He teaches us that Moses and Korach do not just resemble Cain and Abel, but *are* Cain and Abel. The conflict indeed was left unsettled and required a reprise of their roles at a later time in history to settle the matter once and for all.

However, even with this explanation of what Korach 'took' and what Cain 'said', the Talmud still seems to be confused about the value of Moses's and Abel's approach. The dispute is clearly a philosophical disagreement about man's role vis-à-vis the Creator. Cain felt that it was man's right to use his intellect to be the driving force in the relationship between man and God. Hence, without being told, Cain initiates the giving of a sacrifice, while Abel only offers an unsolicited sacrifice as a reaction to Cain's bold move. And when Cain brings a sacrifice, he makes it his duty to bring it from agricultural components so as to attempt to repair the ground's relationship with God. (During the days of creation, the ground had erred and incurred God's wrath). Abel, however, respects God's opinion of the ground and decides not to make any political statements with his offering, but to make it a simple sign of affection. Cain sees man's role as a dominant one. Korach too, feels that if human intellect dictates a logical deviation from a precept, then that deviation should take precedence to the Written Law. After all, in an apparent word for word contradiction to the message of *techelet*, Moses himself says, "It [the Law] is not in heaven ... nor is it across the sea ... rather it is in your mouth and your heart ".[6]

In combining Cain and Korach, Abel and Moses, we seem at one point to have delineated the battle lines, then at the next to be left groping for an understanding of the verdict. The Talmud's question still stands, "Of what benefit is *techelet*?" Why did God tell Cain it is within his power to rule over his destiny and then put down Korach's attempt to empower every individual with the gift of direct connection to God?

There is one detail in the Korach story which does not parallel the Cain and Abel story, but rather finds its comparison in Abraham's ordeal. While Moses implores God not to listen to the rebellion, he throws in what seems to be an unprovoked defense. Moses, like Abraham, finds it necessary at this point to distance himself from any appearance of thievery. Moses says, "I have not taken even a single donkey of theirs".[7] Here Moses finds it necessary, in fighting for the *techelet*, to utilize the same traits that caused God to grant the commandment in the first place. Abraham received the *techelet* for not taking a single thread that did not belong to him. Moses assumes the right to fight for *techelet* because he too has not taken a single donkey that was not his.

Both men were entitled to the articles in question. Abraham had every right to keep the spoils of war, and Moses could have easily rationalized the use of a modest portion of the community resources as leader. Yet they both resisted the temptation to 'take'. They recognize a double standard of sorts. When it comes to others, both men would stop at nothing to protect and defend. When others were in danger or in need, they did not turn away and evoke the idea that God will provide. They took matters into their own hands and prevailed. If this sort of activism does not stem from wholly pure motives, it will manifest itself inevitably in selfish pride. The same zealousness that Cain exhibited with his sacrifice later led him to cold-blooded murder. While Abraham was able to aggressively stand up for others, he showed no such initiative when offered personal compensation.

The *tzitzit* — comprised of a majority of white threads with only a solitary *techelet* thread per corner — represent man's responsibility to himself and the world at large. The color white is the reflective representation of all the colors, and therefore represents all of mankind. When dealing with your fellow man, there must be no excuses. His welfare is firmly within your grasp. As Moses directs us, "It (the Law) is not in heaven ... nor is it across the sea ... rather it is in your mouth and your heart".[8] Preserving life takes precedence over the dictum of the Law. The corners of the garment cannot confine us. We must burst forth as combatants on the battlefield. Each of us must rise to the occasion and assume full responsibility for the human condition. As it says, "Every generation that fails to build the Temple is counted as if it destroyed it".

When it comes to ourselves however, we must look to the lone, dyed thread. Its color, as we mentioned in the beginning, reminds us that between us and God their is a great expanse. An expanse as wide as the oceans, as high as the sky, and as deep as the ever-expanding universe. We must recognize our place in the cosmos and be humbled by it.

The trait expressed by Abraham, perfected by Moses and personified by the *tzitzit*, is the ability to be ever mindful of our diminutive stature; to be greatly humbled by God's great powers — but ultimately deny the urge towards full paralysis; find the strength to stare down the great abyss and persevere. We can be humbled by our ephemeral existence and still find the strength to challenge the infinite expanse.

Before Abraham, man was either a Cain or an Abel. A person's fringes would have been either all white or all blue. Cain went on to build great cities and presumably lead a very productive life. In his incarnation as Korach, we are told that he was one of the wealthiest men ever to live. It was inconceivable to Korach that Moses could be so powerful without an equal measure of selfish pride. Hence he mocked Moses with the all-*techelet* garment. In reality, Moses was called the humblest of all men,[9] yet when it came to saving the Jewish nation, he had the strength to stand up to Pharaoh, wage wars, wrestle the Law away from the angels, and even argue with God Himself!

The portion of the Talmud in which we began our discussion and which left us in slight limbo appears in greater detail in another section of the Talmud.[10] There we find the path from *techelet* to God lengthened by an additional obstacle. There it states, "*Techelet* resembles the sea, which resembles the heavens, *which resembles the sapphire stone*, which resembles the Holy Throne". More importantly, the discussion doesn't end there. It expands upon the role of thievery, which we have established as the root of selfish intentions, and then dives right into a measure of man's humility. It claims that Abraham showed enormous humility by comparing himself to dust and ashes, but that Moses eclipsed all in humility, by referring to himself as 'nothing at all'.[11]

We see from the progression in the Talmud that *techelet* is the appropriate reward for the uncanny ability to be both a strong warrior and a humble servant. As Rebbi Elay teaches at the conclusion of our topic, "The world is suspended on those who can remain silent while engaged in strife".[12]

Techelet, then, focuses us on humanity's power to fight to do good, to fight within the social sphere against tyranny and oppression. In the man-made world within God's creation, man must act, but he must act for others. Thus, *techelet* stands for restraint within the sphere of action represented by the *tzitzit*. It represents action tempered by humility, action for the good of all, rather than for the good of one alone.

The dye necessary to generate *techelet* has been lost to the world since the destruction of the Second Temple. Although some believe it has been rediscovered, Rabbi Yitzchak Luria maintains that the addition of *techelet* to our otherwise all-white fringes is only necessary while the Temple stands. While early generations produced either Cains or Abels, from Abraham until the destruction of the Temple there existed men capable of being both Cain and Abel. Perhaps our generations can no longer produce men with sufficient character to be ranked at all. There is no fear that apathetic modern man will be so proactive, that he will require the *techelet* to rein him in. Until society finds the strength to take a real stand against evil, there is no need to remind us that we are but a spec in the infinite expanse. We fail to act like anything but.

If anything, our post-Holocaust existence requires a *techelet* of a different shade. While the bluish *techelet* of the Torah resides at the far end of the color spectrum, holding our passions in check, our *techelet* might as well be fashioned from fiery red, so it can awaken the true glory that resides within every man.

The word '*techelet*' stems from the word '*tachlit*', meaning the end or ultimate goal. Therein it defines mankind; simultaneously the last to be created, and the purpose of all creation.

Unscathed

The Torah tells us that when Moses ascended the mountain to wrestle the Law away from the celestial beings, he seemed to tarry. With what appears to be tremendous haste, the Jewish people waste no time appointing a new leader. This time however, it is an idol! Understandably, the Lord is infuriated, and informs Moses that his people are a brazen bunch, and He disowns them. Instead, a nation will arise from Moses himself and begin a glorious new people. Moses persuades God to abandon such ideas, and successfully heads back down the mountain, tablets in hand, toward the now frenzied mob.

The full story of the Golden Calf is a bit more complex. It's time to put away the broad strokes and pay attention to the fine details. There is no need to resort to the psychological frailty of this newly freed nation for excuses, the empirical facts of the case are enough to rouse our sympathy.

Firstly, Moses told them he would return in forty days ... he didn't (he meant forty full days). Confusion and doubt began to set in. Satan couldn't let the opportunity pass without a little mischief of his own. For some reason God allowed him to add outright deceit to their understandable confusion.[1] The patch of sky above the people's encampment began playing a celestial apparition of a funeral procession. The obvious conclusion — not only was Moses late, he was no longer! Their greatest fear was now confirmed by visual evidence.

In spite of all this 'proof' the people still refuse to fully accept the obvious conclusion. When they turn to Aaron for assistance they do not claim Moses is dead, rather they profess ignorance as to Moses's whereabouts. The nineteenth century sage Chassam Sofer asks the obvious question: why did the people pretend not to know when they clearly saw their leader's bier?

I'd suggest they were admitting once and for all that man is simply incapable of processing the data he is presented with. This generation had literally seen it all. They had even seen what was normally heard! "And the entire nation saw the sounds".[2] In order to test such a prophetic people the test must somehow completely suspend them between faith and reason.

Without any apologies or regret, divine subterfuge is promoted in broad daylight and in good conscience. The clearest example of reality as ruse is spoken of in Deuteronomy, where God warns the people not to be swayed by false prophets. "If a prophet, or one who foretells by dreams, appears among you and announces to you a miraculous sign or wonder, and if the sign or wonder of which he has spoken takes place, and he says, 'Let us follow other gods' (gods you have not known) 'and let us worship them', you must not listen to the words of that prophet or dreamer. The Lord your God is testing you to find out whether you love Him with all your heart and with all your soul".[3]

God admits that the false prophets may be allowed to sway us by performing miracles and wonders, yet their efforts are only meant to confuse and confound and thereby test man's resolve.

The Holocaust does not have to be understood or embraced under the umbrella of theological reasoning. It can stand as a contradiction to all we hold dear. The point is that we continue to hold on, and in doing so admit that we 'do not know' why six million perished, but our ignorance is not an excuse to abandon, instead it must embolden.

In the case of the delay of Moses, we find an ultimate breakdown in the people's resolve, and if it weren't for Moses's heroism in response to their sin the Jewish people would have been annihilated.

As Moses nears the camp, his initial sympathy for their situation seems to waver. The intensity with which they are celebrating their new-found deity overcomes him, and instead of delivering the precious hand-carved-by-God-Himself Tablets of the Law, he decides to shatter them.

The Talmud takes the trouble to point out that Moses did not consult God, and that his decision to destroy the holy tablets was his own. The Rabbis conclude that God agreed with Moses's reaction and it pleased the Lord. In fact, the last verse in the entire Torah says, "And by all the strong hand and awesome power that Moses performed before the eyes of all of Israel".[4] Rashi comments that this is a reference to the breaking of the tablets. So praiseworthy was Moses's act, that the last word concerning Moses is in praise of this destructive behavior.

The *Midrash* takes the blame slightly off Moses's shoulders by claiming that the hewn letters bid a hasty retreat at the sight of the spiritual carnage. With the letters on their way back to heaven, the blank stone grew exceedingly heavy and could no longer be held by Moses.

If indeed the tablets became too heavy for the mighty Moses, why is he showered with praise for simply dropping them?

The Chassam Sofer, explains the incident in a rather remarkable way. He says that Moses not only threw down the tablets intentionally, but he did so in a manner that would incriminate himself and cause him to be cut off from the Jewish people! Moses saw the letters retreating and realized that in spite of his successful negotiations on behalf of the Jewish nation, they were again in jeopardy of being annihilated. He therefore took desperate measures and intentionally shattered the holy tablets. By doing so, says the Chassam Sofer, Moses was making himself a sinner and unworthy of being the father of a new nation. He was forcing God to make do with the nation he had! Moses was prepared, not only to die for his people, but to sin for his people!

When the nation sins, the letters bid them farewell. However, when sins are committed against the nation, even when the very parchment is being consumed, the letters remain as beacons of hope and guidance.

Lots

There are many ways to understand the events that befall man, and yet there is no way to fully comprehend even the simplest occurrence. One of the starkest examples of the incomprehensible of course, is the Holocaust. Many seek answers to the dilemma that is genocide. Ultimately however, all explanations will fall short, all tongues become tied, and lips sealed at the apprehension of such calamity.

Perhaps the greatest embodiment of this deafening silence can be found concerning Moses's brother, Aaron. After the loss of his two sons, the Torah tells us he was 'silent'.

It is on the heels of the death of Aaron's sons that one of the most bizarre rituals in all of Judaism is introduced. At the height of the Yom Kippur service, two goats are prepared as offerings, but only one is offered in the Holy Temple. The other is selected by lottery to be sent as an offering to '*Azazel*'. It is only when this latter goat is sent on his way that a crimson string suddenly turns bleach white, signifying total forgiveness of the entire Jewish Nation.

The most obvious message would be that life and death are completely arbitrary. These goats are identical in every way, and we make no effort to differentiate between the two. We do not subject the animals to a battery of tests to determine the most worthy; no race is run to determine the fastest; no maze constructed to prove the smartest; no burden brought to select the strongest. By the luck of the draw alone, one serves God while the other does not. Merit, it seems, plays no role before God.

When the wicked Haman wanted to prove that life was chaotic and lacked purpose, he drew lots to establish the day upon which genocide would take place. Haman was determined to relegate what he thought would be the most significant day in the history of the Jewish people to a completely random selection. Similarly, the Nazis sent a chilling reminder of life's haphazardness by condemning millions of innocents to the gas chambers with the flick of a finger.

On rare occasions we find nature itself rise up in protest against what it perceives as intolerable injustice. (Abel's blood rose up in protest when Cain slew his brother; Bilaam's donkey voiced her objection to Bilaam's insistence that it proceed). The *Azazel* offering could very well qualify as a ritual in need of an objection. There of course is no record of a goat rejecting its fate and refusing his designation towards *Azazel*. There is, however, a bull in an unrelated *Midrash*[1] which offers us a glimpse from the point of view of the offering.

In his battle to rid the Jewish people of the influences of idol worship, Elijah the Prophet challenges the idolators of his time to a show-down. Both parties are to offer their respective deities a sacrifice without fire. The offering ignited by heavenly means would be considered the victor.

It all seems pretty straightforward, and the people have their hearts set on a clear revelation of the truth. However, a funny thing happens on the way to the altar — the bull being brought for the idol offering won't budge. This may seem natural, given the fate that awaits him, however, what comes next defies all expectations. In front of all the people assembled, the bull voices his reluctance! "My brother and I have come from the same belly ... yet he has fallen to the lot of Him who is everywhere, and the Name of the Holy One will be sanctified in him, while I have fallen to the lot of *Baal* to provoke my creator".

With some assurance from Elijah, The bull finally understands that his sacrifice will also benefit God and he agrees to participate. However, his original outrage remains a clear expression of the injustice inherent in the selection-by-lots process. Allowing lots to determine one's fate seems to be an affront to nature itself. Even an animal can recognize the injustice in such a system.

So to recap: In front of the entire Jewish Nation, on the holiest day of the year, we take two identical goats, cast a lottery and make one holy and the other — well, other! Could this possibly be the intended message of the Yom Kippur service?

When Albert Einstein was introduced to the findings of Niels Bohr concerning the indeterminacy in quantum mechanics, he refused to believe the theory. His response? "God does not play dice with the universe!" To which Bohr is reported to have retorted, "Stop telling God what to do". It would seem that not only does God play dice, but His dice are loaded!

As it turns out, the random nature of the *Azazel* offering is not even the worst of it all. The real diabolical nature of this offering cuts even deeper into our sensibilities.

As the Chassam Sofer points out, the goat whose lot is for *Azazel* is actually granted an elevated state over his twin. "And the he-goat designated by lot for *Azazel* shall stand *alive* before God".[2] The one full of sin shall remain *alive*, and for the time being, well, while the goat 'lucky' enough to have received God's lot has his neck slit and lies dead on the Temple floor.

Our understanding of the *Azazel* offering has taken a turn for the worse. Another quick recap: We have gone from the horror of an existence that is absolutely arbitrary, completely unpredictable, and devoid of any

possible direction, and entered a maddening reality that not only allows evil to exist, but fosters and nurtures it. Our original fear that we are living in a Godless universe has been replaced with the terror of a universe run by the devil himself.

Something must be missing. There must be a detail, an ending perhaps that sets everything right. What cataclysm eventually befalls this goat of *Azazel*? God directs the *Kohen Gadol* to "send the he-goat to the desert".[3]

And then?

Then, nothing. No retribution, no amount of suffering, no manner of slaughter. The goat is simply set free. His luck never seems to run out.

One year the goat for *Azazel* actual found his way back to Jerusalem and was seen strolling the streets of the city. To avoid this mishap, the tradition of tossing the goat off a cliff was instituted. But even this fateful end was not allowed to be part of the lesson of the *Azazel* offering. No individual was permitted to witness the demise of the goat. Even the lone messenger, entrusted with the task of leading the goat out into the desert, was a person of unique standing. Through divine guidance, the person selected for the job was always someone destined to perish within the year. (In Jewish Law a terminally ill life is in many ways considered to be already dead). Therefore, in essence, there is never a living witness to the fate of the *Azazel*.

Dare we recap? Dare we go on? The more we uncover the darker it gets. *Azazel* erodes every last remnant of hope while it reinforces every agnostic dream. And the Jewish people must endure this affront on a yearly basis, during the holiest day of the year, in the holiest place on the planet.

What sleight of hand can be offered by the Rabbis to set our world back on its axis? What spin can prevent us from careening off our religious bearings?

Thankfully, there is no respite at all!

For if there was a tightly knit resolution underlying the *Azazel* episode, where would we turn for sympathy when our lives encounter the inevitable absurdity?

The *Azazel* solves no dilemma, offers no answers. It is simply the quintessential question. It is every pogrom — every crusade — it is the Holocaust.

When evil rains down upon the earth, one lightning rod simultaneously attracts and grounds each thunderous bolt. *Azazel* as the incarnate of injustice manages to deflect man's existential angst. It exposes the incoherent equation that is faith: G = g ≠ e = G (Where G stands for God, g for good, e for evil) and lays it bare for all to see. The two goats pay homage to the same God just the way good and evil are both manifestations of the One God.

In this way the Holocaust poses no more of a threat to one's faith than does the sacrifice of *Azazel*. By allowing *Azazel* to stand as an unsolved conundrum, God frees man of the responsibility to make sense out of the nonsensical. Try as we may, the empirical world, like *Azazel*, will never add up. Like *Azazel*, the one plus one does not equal two different gods, only one. So too the existence of good and evil does not intimate the existence of two separate gods, or none at all. The same God that accepts the two goats is the same God that bestows goodness and imparts evil.

It is precisely this lesson that rests at the heart of the *Yom Kippur* service. A lesson that can only be taught on the holiest of days. A day when the people are compared to angels and their sins are washed away. In this moment of intensified rapture between the Jewish people and their beloved God; while they remain tightly embraced in a loving bond, they can accept what they cannot comprehend. There is no need to see God's face when you can feel His embrace. As the philosopher Søren Keirkegaard contends, "Does the loving bride in the embrace of her beloved ask for proof that he is alive and real?".

An allusion to the centrality of the lottery to the theme of *Yom Kippur* can be found in the very name of the day. It is called the 'Day of Apparent Lots', *Yom K'pur*. (*Yom* means day, while *Pur* means lots, as in *Purim*) Ultimately, however, the most important part of the day's name is the 'K' of *Yom K'pur*, which means, 'like'. Because ultimately we know that life is anything but arbitrary. The lots drawn are indeed divinely decided. *Azazel* stands in the shadow of our rock solid faith in a God who supremely cares and leaves nothing to chance. As the liturgy of the day proclaims, "You are judge, admonisher, knower, and witness: You inscribe, seal, record and count, and recall all … who shall live and who shall die … who by water and who by fire; who by sword and who by beast; who by hunger and who by thirst … [and ultimately] who will be uplifted".[4]

On the Day of Atonement, our forgiveness hinges on our ability to stand by and witness apparent injustice, without losing our faith in a just God. For this act of heroism, our sins are wiped away. Our ability to remain faithful in the face of the Holocaust should similarly wipe our slates clean.

Grasping

Whatever you do, do not say: 'water, water'![1] That was the only advice offered by the great Rebbi Akiva to his three fellow travelers as they entered the *Pardes* (orchard). As it turns out, that was not quite enough to protect them from harm. Ben Azzai took one look and perished. Ben Zoma went mad, and Aher (Elisha ben Avuyah) lost his faith.

What or where is *Pardes*? It is not clear, but consensus[2] says it was a state of spiritual enlightenment. The four men embarked upon a journey beyond the limits of human comprehension. As it turns out, it was a suicide mission (physically, mentally or spiritually) for all but one of them. Only Rebbi Akiva was able to return in peace.

The specific details surrounding this ill-fated expedition are few and cryptic. Besides Rebbi Akiva's warning, we are told that the object they will misinterpret for water will be a translucent slab of marble. Concerning Ben Azzai and Ben Zoma nothing more is divulged. In Aher's case it says that he took notice of the angel named Metatron, perched atop a glorious throne, and immediately Aher assumed that God is not one but two. He abandoned his faith in God, and never returned.

There is evidence to suggest that *Pardes* is not a destination or a state of mind, but simply an acronym for human comprehension. In Hebrew the word is comprised of the first letters of the four levels of understanding: '*Peh*' for *Peshat* or simple interpretation, '*Reysh*' for *Remiz* or hints, '*Daled*' for *Derush* or extrapolation, '*Samech*' for *Sod* or secrets.[3]

Furthermore, when it comes to Aher's heresy, we find real world causes for his abandonment. One such story[4] has Aher witness a man climb a palm tree on the Sabbath — a violation punishable by death — take the mother bird, along with its young, and descend in safety. At the end of the Sabbath he sees another man who waited until the Sabbath had passed to climb to the top of the same palm tree. The second man follows the biblical command to send away the mother while taking the young, only to be killed by a venomous snake on his way down. Other versions substitute the man with a boy, who is observing the command of his father, while sending away the mother bird. Even though both honoring one's parents and sending away the mother bird are explicitly mentioned as life-prolonging commandments, the boy falls to his death.

Perhaps neither Ben Azzai or Ben Zoma were done in by the supernatural. Perhaps the *Pardes* they entered was not a subconscious trance. On the contrary, their spiritual stature simply reached a level where they became painfully aware of the madness known as the human condition, a condition whose every contradiction and anomaly intensifies as one becomes more aware of it.

This is evident from the greatest prophet of them all: Moses. One would think that at the apex of his interaction with the Almighty, all his questions would feel resolved and an enlightened harmony would reign supreme. Instead, we find Moses moved to such disturbance that he must present God with a provocative question. What of the human condition? Why is it that the righteous suffer while the wicked prosper? Why should a man desecrate the Sabbath by climbing a palm tree and successfully elude the viper's bite, while another waits until after the Sabbath and is smitten? Why should a child obey both his father on earth and his Father in heaven through a single act, and in that very instant perish?

It seems clear that the more one sharpens his focus on comprehending the world at large, the more the lines begin to blur. If ignorance is bliss, the *Pardes* must be sheer torture.

Yet for the believer, the *Pardes* is unavoidable. The day of reckoning will come sooner or later, and whatever you do, "do not say, 'water, water'!"

When a story of such proportion (what I call, deeply shallow, for the presented information does more to further the intrigue than it does to explain it) presents itself, you can leave it to the mystics or take what you can.

I believe a short detour may shed

the necessary light on Rebbi Akiva's warning. There is a fantastic account of a dispute between Reb Eliezer and the Rabbis concerning the susceptibility of a certain type of oven to impurity.[5] A battle ensues wherein Reb Eliezer musters the forces of nature in his defense. He first calls on the deep-rooted Carob tree to uproot itself and transport to another location — the Rabbis are unimpressed. Then he forces a river to flow backwards upstream — this is still not convincing enough. The very walls of the study hall begin to fall in on the Rabbis until Rebbi Yehoshua forbids them to fall any further — threatening but not persuasive. Finally a voice bellows out from the heavens declaring Reb Eliezer correct in his decision — irrefutable but unsatisfying. Rebbi Yehoshua remains firm and proclaims, "The Law is no longer in heaven!" Reb Eliezer must accept defeat.

The question becomes, who was 'really' right? Could heaven have gotten it wrong? *Tosfos* does suggest that the heavens only spoke out of respect for Reb Eliezer, indicating that they may not have actually held that way.

However, later on we are told that God Himself admits to defeat in this matter. Could God have been wrong? If not, then are the Rabbis in error?

The real question is, what is reality? According to Einstein's *Theory of Relativity*, there is no universal reality. Reality is relative to the position of the observer. What is 'real' on earth may not be 'real' in heaven. Two realities can and do exist. The Law was given to man and therefore subject to his sense of reality. The Rabbis couldn't care less what heaven thought of this oven. They calculated the impact such an oven has on the mortal man and

ruled accordingly. Just because the heavenly creatures could apprehend aspects about this oven that made it impervious to impurity, that does not mean that we are able to pick up on the same details. From our vantage point this oven looks like a regular oven and is therefore subject to the same laws as a regular oven. Hence, this oven is both susceptible to impurity and not.

If you think we are slipping into a rabbit's hole, just you wait, we've only begun. Einstein's *Theory of Relativity* can only take us so far. It explains the existence of alternate realities, and provides a framework from which we can appreciate the subjective nature of reality. However, it cannot address the existence of a multiplicity of realities within the same orientation in time and space. Our experience of reality not only differs in kind from that of the *Pardes*, but it also differs in number. While the *Pardes* contains a single strain of reality, wherein all is perfect and good, the human condition contains multiple strains of reality which conflict and contradict each other.

When Rebbi Yehoshua proclaims, "The Law is no longer in heaven!" it is not just a matter of jurisdiction. Once it leaves heaven, it enters the physical world and is subject to our laws of nature. Laws which, we will see, have very peculiar characteristics. Therefore, while all that emanates from heaven is good, not all that arrives on earth is pleasant. The existence of a harmonious reality in heaven does not prevent earthly reality from degenerating into an incoherent nightmare. God's beneficence can appear downright ruthless.

The laws of physics, which support the existence of both good and evil, are found in the theories of quantum mechanics. In a lecture given by A. Oppenheim[6] our case of the oven is cleverly interpreted along the lines of quantum theory. Oppenheim compares our oven to Schrodinger's Cat. In his [Schrodinger's] famous thought experiment, a cat, poison and a radioactive particle are locked in a box. The particle has a 50% chance of decaying. If it decays, it will release the poison and kill the cat. According to quantum mechanics the cat is both alive and dead before we look in the box. Common knowledge would say the cat is either alive or dead, and when we look in the box we uncover what has already occurred. But according to the quantum doctrine, both possibilities coexist until

we make an observation and force the possibilities into a single outcome.

When my wife and I were expecting our first child, some tests indicated that the baby was possibly the victim of a genetic disorder. The doctors wanted to perform an *amniocentesis* to verify their suspicions. There was nothing medically that could be done to change the outcome, but the test would have put our fears to rest if it came back negative. The *halachic* ruling we received was straight out of Schrodinger's notebook. "So long as you don't perform the test, your prayers can still affect the outcome". How can this be? Prayer is invalid if it is done to change something that has already occurred. Either our baby has an extra 18th chromosome or it doesn't. It would seem to be too late to pray. Unless — the *Halakhah* embraces the quantum factor and acknowledges the simultaneous existence of contradictory possibilities.

When Rebbi Akiva warns us not to say, "water, water" he is telling us the trail through the *Pardes* is way, way, off the beaten path. The multiplicity (the existence of both, good and evil) we have become accustomed to, and which at times drives us to the brink of insanity, is a phenomenon built into the matrix of the physical universe. Our perception of evil as a manifestation of God's influence only entered existence when man ate from the Tree of Knowledge between Good and Evil. Rebbi Akiva's doubling of the word 'water' is a reference to our earthly perspective of God as both beneficent and malevolent. Rebbi Akiva calls such a doubling a lie in the *Pardes* because in the rarefied ether of the *Pardes* the laws of quantum mechanics which permit multiplicity — break down. There we must embrace not only the notion, but the reality, that God is One.

On earth, God can appear bipolar if not completely schizophrenic. The assault launched upon our sensibilities by the presence of incomprehensible evil is acknowledged by *Halakhah*. The *Halakhah* recognizes our inability to harmonize good and evil and sanctions our shortsightedness. This concept is best exemplified by the blessing made over bad tidings, which differs from the blessing proscribed for good tidings. When one hears of a tragedy, he must say, '*Baruch Dayin emet*' (Blessed is the true Judge). However, when one wants to express gratitude, the formula is

'*Hatov u'Mativ*' (Blessed is the Good, Bestower of good). In the future, when the age of the Messiah comes, as well as in the *Pardes*, the same blessing of '*Hatov u'Mativ*' will be offered regardless of the tiding.[7]

In *The Knowing Heart*, the Ramchal, Rabbi Moses Chayim Luzzatto, describes the dichotomy between heaven and earth at great length. Without the benefit of the scientific breakthroughs of the last century, he was able to imagine and comprehend the very issues we have been discussing. In the Ramchal's words, "The Blessed One is elevated and exalted above all thought and conception, and possesses not a single one of the properties of His creations ... for anything found in His creations — good or bad, perfection or imperfection — is entirely new, invented by the will of the Blessed One, adapted entirely to our intellect and station, and reflective in no way of the intelligence and essence of the Blessed One".[8]

Our quest to understand the existence of both good and evil in a world run by a single, merciful God, has taken us to the most complicated regions of scientific theory known to man. In fact, the Nobel Laureate, physicist Richard Feynman, went so far as to claim, "I think I can safely say that nobody understands quantum mechanics".[9] It is therefore understandable that persons unfamiliar with the unfathomable depth of the wisdom of the Torah may find it surprising that such esoteric concepts are elucidated in the pages of the Talmud. However, I think it safe to say that even those familiar with the Torah's depth will be impressed with the revelation that our concept of multiple realities, supported by quantum mechanics, can be found, not only in the Talmud, but in a simple nursery rhyme, far from the realm of mysticism and Kabbalah!

"*Ehad Mi Yode'a?*" is a rhyme found in the *Haggadah*, at the end of the Passover *Seder*. The first two stanzas seem quite innocent, but according to the insight of the Chassam Sofer, they explore the very quantum multiplicity inherent in our physical world:

> *"Who knows one? I know one:*
> *One is our God in heaven and earth.*
> *Who knows two? I know two:*
> *Two are the tablets of the Law; One is our God in heaven & earth".*

Says the Chassam Sofer, "The word that emanates from the Almighty is a single merciful utterance. However, when man hears it, the *one* is broken into *two* — containing both mercy, in the guise of the positive commandments, and justice, via the negative commandments".

God is one in heaven and on earth, but He is easily perceived as a multiplicity. It is a real challenge for the mortal mind to fully embrace the belief that both justice and mercy emanate from one God. This challenge is clearly expressed in the twice daily recitation of the *Shema* prayer. *Shema Yisroel, HaShem* (Merciful One), *Elokaynu* (The Lord of Justice), *HaShem Echad*! (are both the Merciful One).

'*Ehad Mi Yode'a?*' exposes quantum mechanics in just the first two stanzas. Imagine what knowledge lies in the remaining eleven!

Water is the perfect analogy for this slippery stance man must maintain as a mortal being. Water has no real shape of its own. Rather it assumes any and all shapes it is put into. Within its fluid form lies the possibility for every shape imaginable. In addition, it can exist as a liquid, solid or vapor! It is the ultimate chameleon and consummate impostor. This lack of integrity has no place in the *Pardes*. In the *Pardes*, when you come upon an impenetrable ocean of water ready to drown you, you must forge ahead undaunted, for the *Pardes* is a parched land without a single drop of H_2O. What appears as an endless onslaught of waves is really an illusion created by the wavy pattern of the solid marble. If we hold on to our earthly prejudices, we will be unable to walk across this rock-solid ocean. Like Aher, we will be fooled into thinking that the multiplicity we experience on earth is also present in the *Pardes*.

While water is the perfect example of our particular form of physicality, Rebbi Akiva is the perfect messenger. He demonstrated throughout his life an uncanny ability to appreciate his vantage point, not deny it, yet remain confident in an alternate reality. This is what gave Rebbi Akiva the strength to laugh at the sight a jackal running through the ruins of the Holy of Holies. Moreover, this is what gave Rebbi Akiva the fortitude to carry on with just five students after his entire life's work, teaching 24,000 students, was wiped out in a plague.

It is this same belief that gives the Jewish people the strength to mourn six million and emerge with faith intact.

B o u n d

O nly a truly stubborn nation could hold steadfast to its tradition and remain solid in its faith, given all the horrors that have haunted the Jewish people throughout the ages.

It is said that much like a blacksmith scorches his iron until it yields to the blows upon his anvil, the Egyptian exile served to mold the Jewish people into a nation. "God has taken you and withdrawn you from the iron crucible, from Egypt, to be a nation of heritage for Him, as this very day".[1] As slaves and sons of slaves, the Jewish people were born of bondage.

The Talmud tells us that a person who remembers the redemption from the Egyptian exile immediately before commencing to pray is worthy of an afterlife.[2] Obviously, our status as a nation is tightly linked to our formative years in the iron crucible of Egyptian bondage. Our dark past not only shaped us, but continues to guide us. It guides us because our salvation from Egyptian whips made us free men, but did not free us of bondage. We remained slaves, but to a new taskmaster. God proclaims: "For it is to Me that the Children of Israel are servants".[3]

The Jewish notion of freedom is a freedom to serve God. The notion that man can be free of any influence at all is foreign to Judaism. As the famed Rabbi Joseph Soloveitchik puts it, "Man who is not bound by any code, who is not subordinate to God, who does not surrender to Him – such a man has not achieved complete humanity. Humanitas in man is completed and perfected by accepting the instructions of God ... [without which, we are in] bondage to our own fears, to our own phobias, to nature, to society, to slogans".[4]

In a world where 'freedom' really means free to be subservient, dare we ask what 'slavery' means? In *Ethics of the Fathers*, the sage Antigonos delivers this maxim: "Be not like servants who serve the master for the sake of receiving a reward, but rather, be like servants who serve the master not for the sake of receiving a reward"[5] While Judaism believes in reward and punishment, Antigonos instructs us to go beyond such motivation. The highest form of servitude is when the servant negates his own interests entirely. He offers his service as a benefit to the master alone. This selfless form of servitude is what the philosopher Søren Kierkegaard refers to in his book *Purity of Heart*. There, he goes so far as to deny the validity of any other form of service on the grounds that, "the man who desires the Good for the sake of the reward does not will one thing, but is double-minded".[6] Such service at best serves two masters — God and the individual — and in most cases the supreme master is the individual's self interest, not God's.

There is an additional implication to Antigonos's aphorism, which speaks directly to our struggles of faith in a post-Holocaust world. Antigonos

teaches us that service and the reward for that service must not be associate partners. Finite man cannot be expected to adequately understand God's infinite wisdom, and connect the dots between service and reward. Such was the dilemma Job faced in his quest to understand the calamities that befell him. God's answer to Job was basically Antigonos's advice: do not focus on reward in this world, God's ways are beyond mortal understanding. Job was a righteous man whose life suddenly came crashing down around him. European Jewry was made up of righteous people whose dynasties were decimated and whose legacies were shattered. Job emerges with his faith shaken, but decidedly intact. God's 'stiff-necked' people not only emerge with a renewed faith of epic proportions, some never even waiver in their devotion.

There is a commandment given to the Jewish people that is meant to provide a physical manifestation of the bondage free-man accepts upon himself. *Tefillin* are bound to the arm and head in a display of subservience. The Torah itself makes the connection between this commandment and our slavery: "It will be as a sign on your arm and an insignia between your eyes, because with a strong hand the Lord brought us out of Egypt".[7]

Our bondage to God is remembered with a binding upon the arm. While our near-extinction, by the Nazis, is commemorated with a branding upon the very same arm. During the Holocaust, concentration camp prisoners received tattoos only at one location — the Auschwitz concentration camp. The first series of prisoner numbers was introduced in May 1940. In order to avoid the assignment of excessively high numbers to the large number of Hungarian Jews arriving in 1944, the SS authorities introduced new sequences of numbers in mid-May 1944. This series, was prefaced by the letter A. Once the number A-20000 was reached, a new series beginning with 'B' was introduced. Some 15,000 men received 'B'

> Well, it may be the devil or it may be the Lord. But you're gonna have to serve somebody.
> - Bob Dylan -

series tattoos. The numbers B-14529 were tattooed on my father's left forearm at Auschwitz-Birkenau.

Beneath our God-given sign, the Nazis provided him with a new sign. This doubly bound arm stands as a clear emblem of our devotion to God. Whether we are being freed from bondage or burned in ovens, our faith does not waver.

When people asked the Satmar Rav for a blessing, he would instruct the seeker to find a person with death camp numbers under his *tefillin*. There, he said, he would find a suitable person to convey blessings.

There are recorded incidents of inmates risking their lives in the concentration camps to don the jet-black straps of the *Tefillin*. Even when deprived of any and all human dignities, man maintains his freedom to serve his God.

L'Chayim

Man's relationship with the Almighty is one that defies all logic. Somehow we accept the possibility that the finite can interact with the infinite, that physical beings can possess a spiritual soul, that our terrestrial actions could have cosmic ramifications. There is no greater delusion of grandeur than man's ability to think he matters. It makes perfect sense that the Catholic Church had a tough time accepting Copernican Heliocentrism in the mid 1500s. And the more we explore the universe the worse it gets. Anxiety over our infinitesimal and even inconsequential standing in the vast universe is unavoidable. When you see illustrations of our very own Milky Way Galaxy, and the neighborhood we inhabit, it is truly humbling to see us way out in the suburbs. Our Solar System doesn't even come close to being the center of our own galaxy, which is itself a relatively tiny member of the greater and ever expanding universe. Throw in some leading theories of 'Dark Matter' 'Dark Energy' and 'Multi-verses' which makes the visible universe only a fraction of what's really out there, and forget about it.

The Rambam advises us to observe the heavens and thereby gain an appreciation for the omnipotent Creator. But doesn't that appreciation come at a stiff price? As an infinitesimal speck on an otherwise unimpressive rock, aimlessly spinning in circles, the last thing I need to do is envision a Creator of such unfathomable dimensions, thereby creating an ever greater gap between Creator and created.

I believe it is this gap that motivates King David in Psalm X, "Why, O Lord, dost Thou stand afar off and hide Thy presence in times of trouble?"[1] Such a stance breeds rebelliousness, as King David continues, "He (the wicked) has said in his heart, 'God has forgotten; He has hidden His countenance; He will never see'".[2] To him, "there is no God".[3] "Successful are his ways in every time, far removed are Your judgments from him".[4] In other words, since Your judgments are far removed from him, he relies on his own way in every instance. In verse thirteen, King David sums up the entire issue. King David asks, "Why does the lawless man mock God?" because, "[h]e says in his heart, 'Thou carest for naught'". And how does King David propose God remedy the situation? "Break the arm of the lawless and the wicked, and when You will search for his evil, You will not find it".[5] It is not the punishment that the lawless require, it is the attention! Grant him that attention, and he will endure all kinds of hardships.

Dr. Viktor Frankl, a survivor of the Holocaust and the founder of Existential Analysis, observed that, "Man is ready and willing to shoulder any suffering as long as he can see a meaning to it".[6]

The generation of the dispersion, who were the builders of the Tower of Babel, fell victim to this malady. Beginning right after the great flood, God instructs Noah to be fruitful and repopulate the earth. According to Rashi, Noah was reluctant to take on the task of repopulation without assurances from God that He would remain hands off and let humanity's efforts succeed. As a sign of His covenant, He shows Noah the great 'bow' in the sky. No longer will the bow face the earth, in the form of divine intervention, but instead, in a gesture of reconciliation, God turns the bow upon himself and vows to leave man in peace.

If we want to fully understand this sign, we have to ask ourselves why God's bow is so colorful. The beautiful symbolism of the rainbow is two-fold. While its positioning shows Noah the non-aggressive stance by God he so desired, its physical properties provides him an even more important message. The rainbow exposes all the hidden colors existing under the veil of white light. When we gaze at the rainbow's full spectrum, we realize that there is always more than what meets the eye. Applying this concept to God, it becomes clear that His involvement in the world is similarly veiled. God's bow will not face us, but His love will never leave us. His glory will exist in every fiber of reality.

Noah accepts God's sign, and with the Creator's weapon turned safely away, man flourishes, and is off to a great start: "The whole earth was of one language, and a common purpose".[7] But things go terribly wrong, and man grows color-blind to the hidden hues of the rainbow. All he sees is the blinding white light. The spectacular color scheme of a life lived with God is no longer visible to his naked eye.

The fantastic rainbow is simply seen as the backwards positioning of God's bow, as King David says, "As the enemies turn backwards".[8] "For the lawless bend the bow; they have prepared the arrow upon the string, that they may shoot in the dark".[9] As man looked skyward and beheld this enormous bow with no sign of an arrow, he took it upon himself to provide the ammunition. God supplied the bow, man would build the arrow. Kabbalistic sources picture the top portion of the Tower of Babel as a triangular shape similar to an arrowhead! It was meant to point heavenward in an obvious gesture of aggression. In the most brazen act of ungracious rebellion, God's sign of goodwill is turned into an instrument of hostility.

What is it about the 'empty' rainbow that provoked such ill will? As we mentioned before, the rainbow was a double sign. God will appear to be hands-off with His creations, yet all the while continue to be intimately linked with them. This is a complicated message, and if a person does not continually reinforce this concept, he will fall victim to understanding only half of the sign. It is not easy to keep in mind that the white light we can see contains within it all the colors we can perceive, and even some we cannot. Just as the colors of

the rainbow appear on only rare occasions — when light can be filtered through drops of rain at precisely a 42° angle — so too, the ability to perceive God's hand in the world is not a task for the faint of heart.

The Tower Builders could not bear the deafening silence caused by their inability to decipher the colors of the rainbow. The rainbow should have reminded them that God is hidden, yet intimately involved in their lives. Instead they only recognized the hidden aspect, and for them, existence without God was madness.

The Torah says very little about the entire Tower incident, but it clearly states their motivation: "And they said, come, we will build for us a city and a tower, whose head may reach unto heaven; and we will make a name for ourselves, lest we be scattered upon the face of the whole earth".[10] The Tower must, 'reach heaven', in order, 'for us to make a name for ourselves'. Why can't it just eclipse the mountaintops and be visible from near and far? If its purpose was to simply keep the people united geographically, the heavens are overkill. And on a purely logical basis, their goal of piercing the heavens cannot be taken literally. Actual studies have been made to determine exactly how high a building could be built before the lower bricks are pulverized by the weight. Heaven is beyond reach. Instead, it is what King David expresses so eloquently — they desperately wanted attention. They wanted God to take notice of

them, and they were prepared to revolt, if need be, to get it. They didn't want to reach the heavens in order to make a name for themselves; they wanted to make a name for themselves so that they could reach heaven!

The alternative for them was "dispersion upon the face of the earth".[11] Social entropy would continue unchecked until man would no longer have any ability to organize and live a life of meaningful existence. All their actions would be merely 'upon the face of the earth', wholly material, entirely transient. Unless they got the attention of their Father in heaven, they were doomed to utter insignificance. Dr. Frankl, calls this an 'existential vacuum'. This vacuum was the experience of a total lack, or loss of an ultimate meaning to one's existence — a meaning, that is, which would make life worthwhile".[12]

The existential vacuum God put in place, is not meant to alienate, but to foster. By restricting Himself and allowing man a foothold, God opens the door to a relationship of co-creators rather than that of creator and created. Without the vacuum, man would not have been made in God's image, he would have been God's image. Man's independence depends on his autonomy, and a relationship between two entities depends on maintaining independence. The minute independence is lost and the two become one, the relationship dissolves. Only as fellow creators can we peer into the heavens, as the Rambam advised, and marvel, instead of recoil, at the sight of God's handiwork.

We are unique among all the creations in the universe. We are created in God's image while all else is God's image. God is one, and man is one-of-a-kind. As the only two unique entities in the universe, God and man seek each other out and find comfort in the other. Only as fellow creators can we expect, and even demand, that God take notice of us. What's more, we can now take notice of God! We can open our eyes and see God returning our gaze. If we renounce our role as creator, we get absorbed into the creation, which is God's image. As God's image our vantage point obscures our ability to look out and see anything.

This is why when God punishes Cain by stripping him of his creative potential, Cain cries out, "and from Your face shall I be hidden?"[13] Cain understood that man's only claim to a relationship with the creator is as a fellow creator. God's punishment was worse than death, it was a complete erosion of any footing from which he could stand in a relationship with God. If Cain could not create then he was a mere creation. This is why Cain becomes fearful that the animals will no longer fear him and kill him, because he is now one of them, "all that find me will kill me".[14]

It is very easy to lose sight of our uniqueness, to ignore our semblance to the image of God, and wipe out any chance we have at relating to the Creator. The vast expanse of utterly empty space stretching billions of light-years in every direction taunts us, belittles us and defeats us. Therefore a reminder of our true exalted state is necessary.

As we have mentioned in the essay titled, 'Confine, Refine, Define', wine plays a pivotal role in Judaism. There we examined its role beyond space and time. But wine also stands for our uniqueness, our being created in God's image, our creative advantage. When we bless the wine, we proclaim God as the creator of the fruit-of-the-vine. But we are not eating the fruit-of-the-vine. We are drinking the squeezed, refined, and fermented juice of the fruit-of-the-vine. For the wine we do not proclaim God as the creator. God's creation ended with the grape. It is man who takes God's grape and creates the wine. By praising God for His part, we are acknowledging a portion that is our part! The blessing over wine affirms our unique status as co-creators.

At a 42 degree angle, the sun's rays can produce a rainbow. As the sun dips past the horizon, its direct influence can no longer be felt, until finally at 18 degrees below the horizon, all manifestation of light is gone. The only way to know the sun still exists is to behold its reflected light through its cosmic emissaries. While the Holocaust conceals the Creator's true identity, it reveals His image in His created ones.

Of course there is plenty wrong with mankind. After all, the same species who survived the camps also built them. But the variety of man that survived did so, and continues to do so, in the image of God. Those who built the camps did so out of cowardice . They built their camps out of the same angst that produced the Tower of Babel. Losing sight of their relationship with the Creator allowed them to exist as mere creations and act as barbaric creatures.

In the words of Rav Joseph B. Soloveitchik zt"l, "But man himself symbolizes, on the one hand, the most perfect and complete type of existence, the image of God, and, on the other hand, the most terrible chaos and void to rain over creation ... man incorporates within himself the most perfect creation and the most unimaginable chaos and void, light and darkness, the abyss and the law, a coarse, turbid being and a clear, lucid existence, the beast and the image of God ... Judaism declares that man stands at the crossroads and wonders about the path he shall take. Before him there is an awesome alternative — the image of God or the beast of prey. It is up to man to decide and choose".[15]

Conclusion

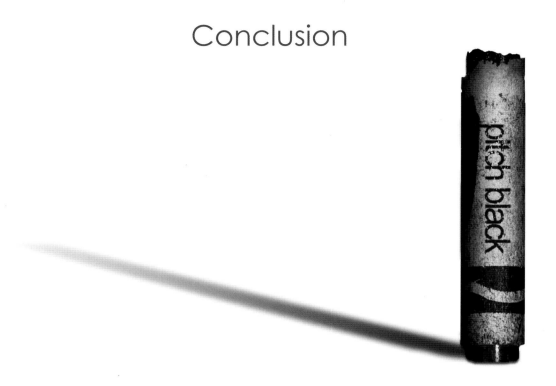

The Sun at high-noon may be the hottest, but it is the setting sun that produces the longest shadows. The generation of the Holocaust was branded by the greatest empire of evil ever to walk the earth. Even as that generation dwindles, the long shadow cast by their oppressors continues to grow. Mankind finds itself groping in the almost pitch black awareness of the absurd madness of its reality. "The Eternal shall smite thee with madness, and blindness, and disquietude of heart: And thou shalt grope at noonday, as the blind gropeth in thick darkness".[1]

Indeed, the existentialist author Albert Camus concludes that; "The modern mind is in complete disarray. Knowledge has stretched itself to the point where neither the world nor our intelligence can find any foothold. It is a fact that we are suffering from nihilism".

The life we have inherited, being lived in the shadow of a devastating Holocaust, is one which defies all reason. When evil can be allowed to express itself with such unabashed vigor, how can existence find any takers? How can a people who witnessed babies being tossed in the air and fired upon for target practice continue to procreate? When the most cultured and sophisticated society on the planet was capable of performing unspeakable human experiments, how can we avoid total anarchy? In an ironic fashion, it is Dr. Joseph Mengele, the notorious 'Angel of Death', who best described

our paradox. Mengele was a medical officer at Auschwitz-Birkenau. In March 1944, a 12-year-old Czechoslovakian boy named Marc Berkowitz arrived at Auschwitz-Birkenau with his mother. As a twin, Mengele chose him for experimentation. He relates: "One morning in July 1944 I spotted my mother among a long line of women moving toward the gas chamber. Mengele called me in and gave me an errand to the crematorium. He knew I would see my mother go to her death. A couple of days later he asked me if I still believed in God".

With prophetic accuracy, the 'Angel of Death' himself provides us with the fundamental dilemma facing all subsequent generations: How can any of us believe in anything? With the devil apparently running the show without any restraint whatsoever, how could anyone still hold out hope for a compassionate God? Yet, based on countless stories of Jews being led to the gas chambers with the song *Ani Ma'amin /I Believe*, on their lips, we have to conclude, much to Mengele's chagrin, that while the Nazi killing machine was highly effective at homicide, it was largely ineffective at deicide.

Without attempting to understand how faith can survive in a Nazi death camp, perhaps we can at least use its implications to our advantage. If the cards are stacked so high in favor of nihilism, then our determination to find some reason to believe is no minor feat. There is a direct correlation between how difficult an event is to overcome and the strength of those able to overcome it. The victims, survivors, their children, and all subsequent generations need to realize that they are not merely victims, survivors, or sons of survivors: they are heroes. Only heroes could come face to face with the devil, stare him down, and remain standing. By all stretches of the imagination, our encounter with the devil should have converted us all into demonic disciples. Our resilience must not be underestimated. We look with an intensity of horror at Nazi atrocities. Should we not show equal amazement at our ability to carry on?

I mentioned in the introduction that, according to the *Maharal* of Prague the best way to understand something is through an analysis of its opposite. Following the *Maharal's* lead, a study of the mechanics behind the miraculous wonder of the Egyptian exodus, will perhaps grant us a glimpse into the far-reaching ramifications of the abominable mystery of the Holocaust.

One of the most miraculous events of the Egyptian exile was the splitting of the sea. The *Haggadah*, which we recite on the night of Passover, debates the number of actual miracles that took place at the Sea of Reeds. It establishes a minimum of at least fifty miracles, five times the wonders visited upon the Egyptian landscape. Yet it is not the miraculous crossing of the sea that matters as much as the lack of miracles on its banks.

As the fleeing slaves approached the sea, they hit a dead end — literally. Their escape had suddenly turned into a trap when their path to freedom ran along the bottom of the sea. Had they taken a wrong turn? Thinking back on the events, it is odd that they were allowed to just stroll out of town in broad daylight. It was almost as if the Egyptians *wanted* them to travel out into the hot, barren desert. In their haste to leave, they hadn't adequately thought things through. Perhaps it was time they more thoroughly assessed the situation. Could the laugh be on them? Had they played right into the Egyptian's hands? Why would God do that?

He wouldn't — but *Baal Tsafon* might!

The Egyptians had erected a massive idol, called *Baal Tsafon/Lord of the North*, way out in the desert. Its purpose was to act as the last line of defense in the event that any slave attempted to escape. Its ominous features would instill fear in the hearts of the bravest of men, let alone a nation of slaves. Had *Baal Tsafon* orchestrated this elaborate turn of events?

Preposterous — all the Egyptian idols were destroyed during the tenth plague. How could a heap of rubble be credited with this final victory?

Not only could it be credited, it was far and away the most plausible answer. It just so happened that their escape route led right to the beachhead of *Baal Tsafon*. Not the *remains* of *Baal Tsafon* mind you, but the fully-intact colossus.

Reports of *Baal Tsafon's* triumph quickly spread near and far. The Egyptian people recognized a change in the tide and without hesitation moved to reclaim their prized possession.

As the sand beneath the feet of the slave nation began to rumble and the thunder of chariots in hot pursuit grew louder, the slaves were overcome by terror. Defeat was a *fait accompli*; death or worse, fast approaching. It is from this fatalistic vantage point that the slave nation made a bold move reminiscent of the faith of the forefathers. In fact, Rashi squarely places this doomed, slave nation on the same level as the great forefathers Abraham, Isaac and Jacob.

What could they possibly have done to earn them such good standing?

What they did, in essence, was walk into the gas chambers with *Ani Ma'amin* on their lips. They faced the *Lord of the North* without turning their backs on God. The vision of a ruthless, unforgiving God, Who now seemed to forsake them, did not fool them for an instant. All might have seemed lost but nothing could be taken away from them. They believed!

Not since long before the first plague had God heard the people cry out to him. "Their outcry because of the work went up to God. God heard their moaning, and God remembered His covenant with Abraham".[3]

Before allowing the people to cross the sea and gain full liberation, God longed for one last expression of faith. It was God's intention all along that this predicament should lead to a genuine cry towards heaven. Their cry was not a grasping at straws made out of desperation, nor was it even a plea for help. It was an affirmation that no matter how dire the circumstances, no matter how hopeless or absurd the situation, the Jewish people still have faith that God is riveted on His people and will never give up on them.

Such devotion can only be manifest when all natural manner of salvation has been extinguished, thus leaving man no reasonable recourse. Under such conditions man will either be gripped by a paralyzing apathy or infused with a passionate faithfulness. Similar sentiments are found in Psalms 92:3 where it says, "Proclaim by day, Your loving-kindness, and Your faithfulness by night". Faith is a matter for the night. That is why the Rabbis compare this world to the night, and our job in this world is not to see the light, or wait for the dawn, but to find the faith within us while gripped by peril and full of trembling.

It is for this reason that Rashi equates the crying out on the banks of the *Yam Suf* to the prayer of the forefathers. Both are born, not out of an appreciation of God's kindness, but out of a recognition of God's omnipotence, out of angst and terror; both are examples of perfect faith.

The lengths to which God had to go to squeeze out a few genuine expressions of love and devotion shows us that the natural tendencies of the people were not on such a high level. In fact they were on the 49th level of impurity out of a possible 50

While the emergence of dry land in the midst of a splitting sea provides the necessary platform for an escape by foot, such a predicament would run a ship aground.

when they left Egypt.

God did not save His people insomuch as He refused to destroy them! In a tirade lasting more than 40 verses in Ezekiel, chapter 20, God bemoans the fact that in the 14th Century B.C.E., during the Egyptian exile, He *had* to save the Jewish people, "I intended to pour My fury upon them ... but I acted for the sake of My Name ... [reluctantly] I took them out of the land of Egypt". The Jewish people were rescued from Egypt in an attempt to avoid a desecration of God's name. If God had forsaken His people, the nations of the world would have had good reason to deny Him.

The question then becomes: if the avoidance of a desecration of God's name could serve as the catalyst for salvation in Egypt, why did such a concern fail to avert the wholesale slaughter of 6,000,000 men, women and children in Europe?

Was the Holocaust any less a desecration of God's name than abandoning the Jews in Egypt would have been?

Why did the sea split for the Jews fleeing Egypt and refuse safe passage for the Jews fleeing Europe?

In May of 1939 a transatlantic ocean liner, the SS St. Louis, sailed from Hamburg, Germany across the Atlantic seeking safe harbor for its almost 1,000 Jewish refugees. When no country, including the United States, would allow the vessel to dock, it was forced to return to Europe where approximately half of its

Where a statue of an ominous Egyptian god stood witness to God's kindness, there now stands the statue of a Roman goddess of liberty, blocking the path to safety.

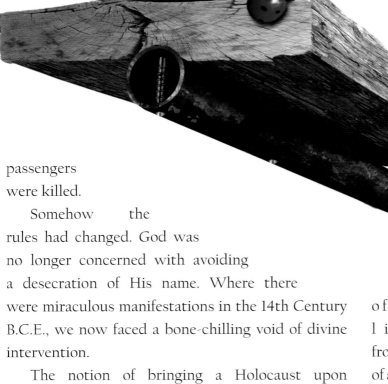

passengers
were killed.

Somehow the
rules had changed. God was
no longer concerned with avoiding
a desecration of His name. Where there
were miraculous manifestations in the 14th Century
B.C.E., we now faced a bone-chilling void of divine
intervention.

The notion of bringing a Holocaust upon humankind must have been at least mentioned, if not hotly debated, in God's heavenly tribunal prior to unleashing the killing machine known as the Third Reich. Why didn't anyone raise the objection, that on the grounds of protecting God's good name, such a cataclysm should be avoided? And if such an objection was voiced, why was it obviously ignored?

It is this question which the entire body of work collected in this bound edition struggles with, and each work of art and thought, in its own way, strives to answer.

The cumulative answer, if it is not yet apparent, is that in Egypt only God could prevent a desecration of His name, while in Europe it was God's people who — by their stubborn refusal to give up — could transform the greatest desecration of God's name into the greatest sanctification. While the Creator Himself can be easily misunderstood by man's finite mind, His creations can serve as a reflection, and offer an interpretation of the true nature of the Holocaust's valuable message. A message of hope, sanctification and love.

When a people can approach their last moments

of
l i f e
from the inside
of a gas chamber and find
the strength to raise their voices
in unison proclaiming their undying faith;
when survivors and subsequent generations can carry on in spite of all the horrors they have witnessed, you are faced with a sanctification of God's name unlike any the world has ever seen.

The Holocaust has placed us back on the banks of the *Yam Suf*, sent us back to the times of the forefathers, squarely within the darkest corner of a long exile.

Fortunately, humankind has developed a keen sense of night vision. Our eyes have become so adept at peering into the abyss that we often have to squint and shield our pupils from any trace of visible light. The *Astyanax Fasciatus Mexicanus* or Blind Cave Fish, would make an appropriate mascot for the human race. Through eons of existence within pitch-dark caves off the Mexican coast, these fish have evolved into eyeless creatures. Yet their lack of optics does not prevent them from 'seeing'. They have developed a light sensitive organ in their brains enabling them a perception of the environment around them.

With wide open eyes and highly dilated pupils,

we perceive the horrors roaming in every corner of our existence, and cling to our faith ever tighter. Blind faith is a senseless groping where images neither help nor hinder. The faith we embrace is one of conflict, contradiction and overwhelming confusion. Like it or not, we see all too well in the dark. The monsters are all too real and the demons all too demonic. Yet somehow, we are able to catch a glimpse of the puppeteer's nylon threads. We are able to discern the jerky, puppet-like movements in the evil before us, directing our search for answers away from the puppets and up towards the Puppet Master Himself.

Indeed, Rav Yerucham Levovitz, (1874-1936), the Spiritual leader of the famous *Mir Yeshivah* in Europe before WWII, believed that as clear as God's manifestation was to pre-sin man, so too is his manifestation to modern generations. As it says, "I am the first and I am the last".[4] As God is in the beginning, so too is He in the end. The difference being that while Adam in the Garden could perceive God's glory as clear and transparent as day, we must be able to perceive Him conversely, through the obscure and the opaque. Our eyes can no

longer process the light of God's presence. We only sense the long shadows and the stifling dread. Somehow God must glow in the dark.

It was the French author Albert Camus who said, "In the depth of winter, I finally learned that there was within me an invincible summer". And the extraordinary Helen Keller understood it most eloquently, "Character cannot be developed in ease and quiet. Only through experience of trial and suffering can the soul be strengthened, vision cleared, ambition inspired, and success achieved".

The mantra for the Holocaust is: 'never forget'. The hope of that slogan is that by remembering, we will see to it that it does not happen again. The logic in a remembrance serving as a future deterrent is questionable, but as a litmus test for determining humanity's ability to triumph over evil, remembering is vital. Without a clear memory of how bad it can get, we have no way of knowing how good we have been. It is as if we are living on some cosmic seesaw. Without a counter-weight to lift us off the ground, we merely grovel in the dust. However, having a counter weight with the critical mass of the Holocaust, we are not just lifted high in the air, but catapulted into the sky. At such heights, even the simplest acts become heroic, making even the simplest of us heroes.

In the shadow of darkness, there exists a great light — the light that shines within us. It is this light, which the body of work titled *Black is a Color* has hopefully managed to illuminate.

Moments after entering the world on March 24th, 1963 in Los Angeles, California, the infant is cradled in his father's arms, the left one tattooed with the concentration camp number B-14529. Eight days later, his godfather tenderly holds the newborn with a similarly branded arm, the number A-11410 clearly visible beneath the intermittent stripes of his jet black *tefillin*. The child's father and godfather stand side-by-side as the child is given the name, Shlomo, in memory of their very own brother, who was shot by a fleeing Nazi guard just one day before the camp was liberated.

Twenty-five years later the child has his own son, and names him Dov, after his murdered grandfather, A-11409, whose body finally weakened during a cruel winter march. His position in line continued receding until he met with the executioner's bullets at the rear of the procession. "How he met thee by the way, and smote the hindmost of thee".

Stan (Shlomo) Lebovic studied at the Corcoran School of Art in Washington, D.C. He has owned several illustrative service companies, and before devoting himself exclusively to *Black is a Color* he published a children's book, which received a Toy of the Year Award and was featured in Disneyworld and on the QVC Television Network.

Upon completion of *Black is a Color*, Mr. Lebovic's spiritual appetite and perpetual existential angst set their sights on what is arguably the most widely read piece of literature in the Jewish world: The Passover *Haggadah*.

Titled *Out of Bounds*, his interpretation of the *Haggadah* has been hailed as a work, "... not only [to] be read but [to] be studied, absorbed and savored ..." Mr. Lebovic has once again exposed us to the richness and extreme relevance found deep within traditional Jewish thought.

His spiritual struggle as a survivor's son has without a doubt molded him, and the art he creates.

"Self-Portrait"

Sharp, dull, pristine or worn, we are all just tools in the Lord's shed.

118

A Haggadah by Stan Lebovic

An Exodus of Existential Proportions

In my father's hometown, Velke Kapushani, in the eastern-most section of the Slovakian Republic, the Nazis seized control on the eve of Passover. The soldiers took up residence within the Jewish homes. It became clear that deportation was not a matter of *if*, but *when*. For some reason, the Germans waited until after Passover to evacuate the Jewish families. That final Passover in 1944 could easily have been the hardest on record, and during the years of the Holocaust, that scene played out in millions of homes. As they chanted, "next year in Jerusalem", most would be happy if next year they were *anywhere*. By the holiday of Shavuot, just seven weeks later, nearly half of my father's family was gassed to death. By the following Passover, only he and two brothers had survived.

The *Seder* night is an opportunity for one generation to pass on its hard-fought faith to the next generation. Throughout our long exile, there have been trying times, as the *Haggadah* foretells, "In all ages they rise up against us to destroy us". No generation can attest to this fact better than one raised in the aftermath of the Holocaust and whose *Seder* nights were led by Fathers and Grandfathers whose arms were tattooed with death camp numbers.

As the living legacy of attempted genocide, we can no longer make do with a casual or superficial reading of the Passover *Haggadah*. There are simply too many questions, too many contradictions and too few faithful. We must lean on the literature as never before, and mine it for all it is worth.

The *Haggadah* must provide more than an affirmation of faith; it must be able to encourage, inspire and above all instill a firm belief in a loving god.

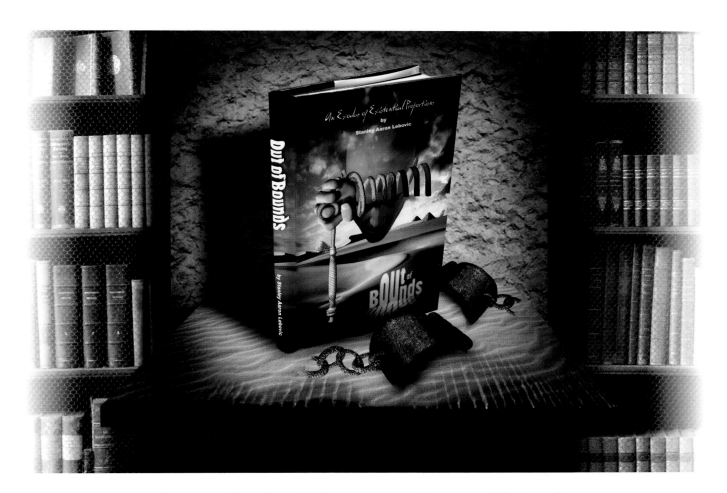

To order a copy of *Out of Bounds* please visit our website: www.blackisacolor.com

Notes

Foreword: 1) Tractate Brachot 4b 2) Tractate Brachot 12b **A Lasting Impression**: 1) Jonah 4:11 2) Genesis 27:22 3) Deuteronomy 32:39 4) Pirke D'Rebbi Eliezer 34:2 5) Genesis 27:16 **Hide & Seek**: 1) Worship of the Heart p. 74 2) ibid p. 75-76 3) ibid p. 77 4) ibid p. 77-78 5) ibid p. 78 6) ibid p. 80 7) Genesis 41:1 **Turn The Page**: 1) Worship of the Heart p. 80 2) Tractate Brachot 32b 3) ibid 4) Tractate Brachot 31b **Broken Glass**: 1) Tractate Brachot 31a, Tosfot 2) Tractate Brachot 31a 3) Tractate Brachot 31a, Tosfot 4) Ecclesiastes 3:4 5) Tractate Brachot 31a 6) Tractate Brachot 28a 7) Psalm 4:7 8) Psalm 4:8 9) Genesis Rabah 19:4-5 10) Tractate Sanhedrin 108b 11) Isaiah 57:20 12) Tanhuma B. Vayikra 13) Tractate Bava Basra 4a 14) Psalm 17:4 15) Tractate Sanhedrin 42a 16) Kings II 20:1 17) Tractate Brachot 10a **Destination Unknown**: 1) Ramban on Genesis 12:6 2) Genesis p. 79 3) Tractate Sanhedrin 102a 4) Kedoshim **Confine, Refine, Define**: 1) Psalm 8:1 2) Genesis Rabah 15:7, 19:1 3) Tractate Brachot 40a & Tractate Sanhedrin 70a 4) In Torah terminology eating includes all aspects of nourishment. cf. Yoma 76a 5) Genesis 3:6 6) Genesis 2:17 7) Husserl Expositions and Appraisals by Ricoeur p. 6-7 8) Genesis 3:8 9) Genesis 2:9 10) Genesis 3:22 11) Genesis 3:17 12) Tractate Tamid 32b 13) Kohellet Rabah 1:34 14) Psalm 8:6 15) Genesis 6:4 16) Genesis 5:29 17) Genesis 9:20 18) Megillat Esther 2:15 19) Megillat Esther 7:7 20) Megillat Esther 4:13 21) Megillat Esther 4:16 22) Halachik Man p. 135, p. 85 23) Will and Representation I, Schopenhauer, p. 178-9 24) Halachik Man p. 46 25) ibid p. 131 26) ibid. p. 99 27) ibid p. 55 **The Covenant**: 1) Hirsch Haggadah 2) Genesis 15:17 3) Zohar Chadash (Genesis 274) 4) Genesis 15:17 5) It is possible that the time in Egypt was far worse than the Holocaust. Even so, in Egypt the Jewish people fell to the lowest level of impurity tolerable. As we will see, that did not happen in the Holocaust. As a result, Abraham's consolation could be found at this juncture. **Baggage**: 1) Tractate Taanis 23a 2) Ecclesiastes 1:3 3) Ecclesiastes 1:4 4) Ecclesiastes 2:18 5) Psalm 126:1 6) Psalm 90:10 7) Tractate Taanis 23a Maharasha 8) Kings II 4 9) Kings II 28 10) Habbakuk 1:2 11) Tractate Taanis 23a 12) Tractate Taanis 24b 13) Psalm 17:14 14) Tractate Shabbos 33b 15) The Challenge of Wealth by Meir Tamari p. 18 16) Tractate Chullin 91a 17) ibid. **Culture Shock**: 1) Genesis 4:3 2) Ramban on Genesis 4:7 3) The Emek Yehoshua 4) Genesis 4:7 5) Genesis 4:10 6) Genesis 4:14 7) Genesis 4:12 8) Genesis 4:13 9) Psalm 8:6 **Apathy**: 1) The Emek HaDavar 2) Tractate Brachot 33b 3) Rashi on Genesis 4:10 quoting Tractate Sanhedrin 37b 4) Tractate Sanhedrin 37b, Tosfos 5) Tractate Sanhedrin 37b 6) Genesis 4:2 7) Genesis 4:10 8) Genesis 2:7 9) Deuteronomy 12:23 10) The Rebel by Albert Camus, p. 24 11) Genesis 4:7 12) Psalm 90:3 13) Psalm 90:3 14) The Rebel p. ix 15) http://www.aish.com/spirituality/philosophy/The_Meaning_of_Adam 16) Ezekiel 16:49 17) Genesis 18:27 18) Genesis 6:9, Rashi 19) The Rebel p. 306 20) ibid. p. 22 21) ibid. p. 28 **Still Life**: 1) http://www.thebigview.com/spacetime/uncertainty.html 2) Jonah 4:11 3) http://www.bbc.co.uk/DNA/h2g2/A408638 **Sticks and Stacks**: 1) Leviticus 26:24 2) ibid. 3) Deuteronomy 28:28 4) Proverbs 31:18 **Lullaby**: 1) Code of Jewish Law: Y.D. 338:1 2) Tractate Zevachim 89a 3) Ecclesiastes 3:1 4) Purity of Heart, Søren Kierkegaard: p. 36 5) Ecclesiastes 3:11 6) Judaism, Human Values, and the Jewish State: p. 13 7) Exodus 25:8 **The Sound of Sacrifice**: 1) Music Made in Heaven by Rav Moshe Eisemann p. 4 2) Tractate Rosh Hashana 16a 3) Highway 61 Revisited by Bob Dylan 4) The Myth of Sisyphus by Albert Camus, p. 35 5) ibid. p.50 6) ibid. 7) ibid. p.54 8) ibid. p.39 9) Halachik Man by Rav Soloveitchik, p.30 10) ibid. p.142 11) Tractate Shabbat 88a 12) Exodus 24:7 13) Genesis Rabah 56:8 14) Genesis 21:12 15) Genesis 22:2 16) Halachik Man by Rav Soloveitchik, p. 143 17) Genesis 22:13 18) http://www.ou.org/chagim/roshashannah/theshofar.html **Cosmic Ash**: 1) Tractate Megillah 6b 2) Genesis 32:25, Baal HaTurim 3) Psalm 118:20 **On Holy Ground**: 1) Exodus 3:2 2) Exodus 3:3 3) Tractate Taanis 21a 4) Tractate Brachot 60b 5) Isaiah 45:7 6) Genesis 22:5 7) See the essay The Sound of Sacrifice for a full discussion of the matter 8) Exodus 3:3 9) Tractate Maakos 24a-b 10) Exodus 3:14 11) Tractate Brachot 12) Exodus 3:5 13) Tractate Yevamos 102b, based on Ezekiel 16:10 14) Tractate Yoma 54a **Bloodshot**: 1) Tractate Sotah 17a 2) Genesis 14:22,23 3) Tractate Sotah 17a 4) Deuteronomy 16:1 5) Genesis 4:8 6) Deuteronomy 30:12 7) Numbers 16:15 8) Deuteronomy 30:12 9) Numbers 12:3 10) Tractate Chullin 89a 11) Exodus 16:7 12) Tractate Chullin 89a **Unscathed**: 1) Tractate Shabbos 89a 2) Exodus 20:15 3) Deuteronomy 13:1-3 4) Deuteronomy 34:12 **Lots**: 1) Kings I 18:20-40 2) Leviticus 16:10 3) Leviticus 16:22 4) The Yom Kippur Machzor during the repetition of the Musaf Shmone Esreh. **Grasping**: 1) Tractate Haggigah 14b 2) Tractate Haggigah 14b, Tosfos 3) The ARI'zl Shaar HaKavonos 4) Tractate Haggigah 14b 5) Tractate Bava Metzia 59a 6) http://www.springbird.net/ 7) Tractate Brachot 60b 8) The Knowing Heart by the Ramchal p. 63-65 9) The Character of Physical Law (1965) **Bound**: 1) Deuteronomy 4:20 2) Tractate Brachot 4b 3) Leviticus 25:55 4) Festival of Freedom by Rav Soloveitchik, p. 50-51 5) Ethics of the Fathers 1:3 6) Purity of Heart, Søren Kierkegaard: p. 69 7) Exodus 13:16 **L'Chayim**: 1) Psalm 10:1 2) Psalm 5:11 3) Psalm 5:4 4) Psalm 5:5 5) Psalm 5:15 6) Confrontation by Zvi Kolitz p. 142 7) Genesis 11:1 8) Psalm 10:4 9) Psalm 11:2 10) Psalm 11:4 11) ibid. 12) Confrontation by Zvi Kolitz p. 141 13) Genesis 4:14 14) ibid. 15) Halachik Man by Rav Soloveitchik p. 109 **Conclusion:** 1) Deuteronomy 28:28,29 2) exodus 6:3 3) exodus 2:23, 24 4) Isaiah 48:12